The Men Behind the Decisions

The Men Behind the Decisions

Cases in European Policy-Making

Glenda Goldstone Rosenthal
New York University

Lexington Books
D.C. Heath and Company
Lexington, Massachusetts
Toronto   London

Library of Congress Cataloging in Publication Data

Rosenthal, Glenda Goldstone.
   The men behind the decisions.

   Bibliography: p.
   Includes index.
   1. European Economic Community countries—Economic policy.
2. Decision-making. I. Title.
HC241.2.R64   338.94   75-4
ISBN 0-669-99325-5

Copyright © 1975 by D.C. Heath and Company

Published simultaneously in Canada

Printed in the United States of America

International Standard Book Number: 0-669-99325-5

Library of Congress Catalog Card Number: 75-4

Contents

Preface

This book tries to supplement the rather meager body of available descriptive and theoretical materials on European Community processes. Existing studies seemed rarely to relate complex theoretical proposals about how European institutions work to the individuals who actually work for the institutions. On the other hand, something more than a series of impressionistic accounts was called for. I therefore attempted to combine political science techniques and journalism, the objectivity of an academic analyst and the insights of a working participant.

Many friends, teachers and colleagues contributed, directly and indirectly to the book. My interest in the European Community was aroused by Henri Brugmans and by a year of study at the College of Europe in Bruges. The late Philip E. Mosely did much to sustain this interest. My dear friend and colleague Donald Puchala was a constant source of ideas, encouragement, and support from the very start of my graduate studies. Other colleagues who gave encouragement and advice include Gordon Adams, Robert Cox, Stuart Fagan, Wilfred Kohl, and Steven Warnecke.

I could not have collected the documentary materials without the aid and cooperation of the European Community Information Service staffs in Washington and New York. My field work in Brussels was made possible in large part by Madeleine Ledivelec. The typescript was prepared by Alice Goldman and the index by Robin Ludwig with the help of a grant from the Institute on Western Europe of Columbia University. Finally, this book could not have been published without the patient, unflagging efforts of my husband, David Ellenhorn, who read the manuscript, commented on it, and suggested many improvements.

1

Decision-Making in the EEC: A Definitional Problem

Although the term "decision-making in the European Community" has been used since the late 1950s, observers have never decided exactly what they mean by it. Analysts are not usually explicit about whether they are referring to a single process or to a whole set of processes; whether they are looking for the people or for the institutions that wield the most power and influence; or what exactly they mean by power and influence in the European Community context.

Ernst Haas points out one of the principal reasons for confusion. The difficulty, he suggests, lies in the

dependence of most propositions on a number of explicit and implicit assumptions made prior to the initiation of research; there is a theoretical basis to the mere listing of variables. The findings are as strong as the assumptions, and the assumptions cannot be made evident without looking at the theories which inspired them. The same is true of the measures and indicators embedded in various assumptions.[1]

This difficulty is closely related to the failure to distinguish between the process and the end product. Analysts have frequently based their observations on the firmly held, but often unstated, belief that "integration" is a desirable end product. Thus, their initial propositions about policies and decision-making are intermeshed with other propositions about some ideal, but only very vaguely defined, future goal. The concern in this book is to avoid the confusion between process and outcome and the tangled discussion of what integration should mean. The aim is to observe, as free from normative considerations as possible, how the European Community has functioned in the past and is functioning now, and thus to arrive at some generalizations about processes and actors.

Although the 1957 Rome Treaty lays down guidelines on decision-making in the EEC,[2] the treaty clearly provides only a framework for what have become, over time, highly complex and very different sets of procedures. This book contends that there is no single decision-making process in the EEC but multiple processes that depend on many different variables. It also contends that there is no single decision-initiating or decision-making body, such as the EEC Commission or the Committee of Permanent Representatives, but groups that shift in response to many different pressures.

For the purposes of this study, the terms *decision* or *decision-making* are to be construed in the broadest possible manner so as to include, wherever possible, all the intricate negotiations in all the groups and institutions involved with a proposal from the time it is broached. Obviously, this involves examining an enormous, unwieldy body of material. The difficulties are compounded by the fact that in many instances EEC records are not public. In other instances, reports of the most crucial phases never appear on paper because the key figures engage in dinner table or cocktail lounge diplomacy. However, some of the gaps can be filled by detailed interviewing and by careful scrutiny of official records, daily press reports, and commentary in the specialized journals.

Decision-making cannot be viewed only as a culminating point when the Council of Ministers meets, often in a marathon session, negotiates a package deal, and votes on it. It must be regarded as a continuum that can extend over a period as long as ten years. At any point along this continuum, pressures can be exerted by a large variety of groups and institutions both from within the Community institutional structure and from outside. Only then is it possible to obtain a clear picture of why the Council finally adopted a particular line of conduct.

Although it is hypothesized that EEC decision-making is a complex, often unique set of processes stretching over a long period of time and involving very many different individuals, groups and institutions, it is not suggested that the processes are random or anarchic and that no generalizations can be made. On the contrary, this study hopes to show that generalizations can indeed be made so long as the analyst develops an appropriate methodology.

Important work in developing a dynamic analytical framework with multiple shifts of perspective has been carried out in the last five years by students of United States foreign policy. In this context, Graham Allison's study of the Cuban missile crisis was crucial to the present analysis, since a number of his ideas have been borrowed to form part of the methodological base. Allison points out:

In attempting to explain a particular event, the analyst cannot simply describe the full state of the world leading up to that event. The logic of explanation requires that he single out the relevant, important determinants of the occurrence.

And, as he suggests earlier: "What each analyst sees and judges to be important is a function not only of the evidence about what happened but also of the 'conceptual lenses' through which he looks at the evidence."[3] Thus, we are back to the Haas proposition referred to earlier: a number of explicit and implicit assumptions are made prior to the initiation of research. Allison makes a very simple and practical suggestion to neutralize this bias. As he showed in detail in the case of the Cuban missile crisis, if we look at a single sequence of events through a number of different conceptual lenses, we are likely to obtain alternative explanations of those events.

Five decisions were used here as case studies. The three main approaches adopted in previous literature on decision-making in the European Community were formulated in terms of conceptual schemes. Each of these three schemes was then applied in turn to the five decisions. Thus, fifteen descriptions of decision-making were obtained. They differed from each other sufficiently to validate the initial hypothesis that no single method can describe all decision-making in the European Community. However, this does not mean that the fifteen different explanations are totally discrete. Quite the reverse. While different from each other in some respects, they overlap in enough areas and often enough to enable a set of tentative generalizations to be formulated.

Conceptual Scheme I: Intergovernmental Politics

According to a number of well-known analysts, national political leaders decide whether matters will be regulated via traditional diplomatic processes or whether they may be discussed and regulated by the institutions of the European Community. The selection will be made in terms of the extent to which "national interests" are considered at stake.[4] The actor in this conceptual scheme is a small group of individuals, usually the foreign ministers of the EEC member countries, sometimes the heads of state or of government and, on occasion, other members of the government, particularly ministers of finance and economic affairs. The decision-making arena may take the form of traditional multilateral diplomatic negotiations; "summit" meetings of heads of member states or governments, held under European Community auspices but independently of formal Community processes; bilateral talks between heads of state, foreign ministers or other government members; or meetings of the Council of Ministers of the European Communities. The process is essentially interactions between a few men, each of whom perceives the defense and, he hopes, the enhancement of his own nation's position as the primary goal of his activity.

Much of the intergovernmental politics literature focuses on the distinction between "high politics" and "low politics" issues. Traditionally, "high politics" issues—national defense, foreign affairs—have been the concern of heads of government and high-ranking cabinet ministers, whereas these men deal much less frequently with "low politics"—social and economic issues. A "high politics" issue, it is asserted, cannot be dealt with outside the framework of the individual member states of the Community, since the nations are far too jealous of their individual "vital" or "national" interests to allow decisions to be made for them by "outside"

(Community) institutions. However, "low politics" questions may indeed by removed from the exclusive preserve of the member states and be regulated by Community bodies, since, it is argued, national interests are not likely to be endangered to any significant degree.[5]

It has been fashionable, particularly since the Community crisis of July 1965 to January 1966, to emphasize the high politics/low politics distinction and to discern a growing assumption of power by the national governments in European Community affairs. This, it is claimed, can be seen from the activities of the experts in the national capitals, in the Committee of Permanent Representatives in Brussels, and in the Council of Ministers of the Communities itself. Clearly, any study viewed through the inter-governmental politics conceptual lens alone would bring out this factor. By turning to the second conceptual lens, a different image is obtained.

Conceptual Scheme II: Grass-Roots, Interest Group, and Parliamentary Pressures

In this scheme, decision-making is the outcome of effective public pressures exercised directly by the public or articulated through interest groups and parliamentary representatives. In contrast with the first scheme, which embraces only a small group of high officeholders, the present one assumes that decision-making encompasses the views, pressures, and actions of what Karl Deutsch has termed "the politically relevant strata of the population at large." This group is

sufficiently accessible, interested, capable, and old enough to have at least a potential influence on politics so that they have to be taken into account in estimating the probable outcome of crisis. The politically effective "people" amounts in Western countries to the total electorate actually voting: that is, to between 60 and 90 per cent of the adult population.[6]

Since all these people do not become mobilized on every issue, another and somewhat more useful way to describe the actors is in terms of Gabriel Almond's concept, developed by James Rosenau: the "attention" or the "aroused" group. These groups, Rosenau explains, are

unorganized segments of the mass public . . . which are normally passive and disinterested, but which acquire structure as an aroused group whenever an issue arises that directly affects their common interest. . . . Their entrance into public debate is then sudden and impulsive, and confined exclusively to the single issue which provoked them. Their recommendations concern only that issue, unmodified by and irrespective of the requirements of any other policy considerations. Once the issue has subsided, these attention groups disband . . . returning to the status of unorganized and passive segments of the mass public.[7]

The decision-making arena here, in sharp contrast once again to the arena sketched out in the first conceptual scheme, can be almost all-encompassing. It extends out from (and, since communication is a two-way process, also centers on) the members of the EEC Commission and their close personal staffs, leading members of the administrative departments, and members and officials of the European Parliament and the Economic and Social Committee of the Communities; to the federations of interest groups (the so-called umbrella groups); and to regional, national and even local subgroups. This somewhat linear representation is made more complex by the need to weave into it the governmental and interest group structures in each of the six member countries of the European Community.

Just as the actors in this scheme can number many thousands or be restricted to a fairly small group of delegates, and the arena can encompass anything from local administrations to a complex amalgam of local, regional, national, and Community institutions, so processes can vary greatly too. They range from local meetings of unions or associations representing one particular interest who wish to have their needs and desires made known on a broader level, to massive assemblies of the large Community-level federations of unions and associations such as the Comité des organisations professionelles agricoles (COPA). The processes may also involve questioning in the national parliaments or persistent watchdog action by a whole group of committees of the European Parliament. They can include too a quiet lobbying visit by an individual representative of one interest group with a member of the EEC Commission or a massive demonstration by 80,000 rioting farmers in the streets of Brussels. In all these ways, grass-roots pressures make themselves felt directly or indirectly.

Conceptual Scheme III: Elite Networks

In this scheme, decision-making is the result of the action, persistence, and determination of a small, closely knit group. In almost every case, the network functions in the interest of a cause. The cause can range from high ideological aspirations, as for example the promotion of greater European unity, to the pursuit of the personal or group ambitions of high officials within the European bureaucracy.

The actors in this scheme are once again a small group of influential men. The group may be composed of one outstanding personality surrounded by a small number of loyal personal aides, or it may be a kind of "old boy" network, groups brought together by the same interests, background, or training. World War II Resistance fighters form a particularly significant "old boy" network in the EEC.[8] Recently, this identity of views seems to have faded as an ideological phenomenon. Many of the men politically active in the 1940-60 era who were old enough to occupy high political positions in the immediate postwar years no longer lead active political lives. Also, the Community is becoming more and more a vast bureaucratic machine with little room for what is regarded by the second generation of Community officials—younger and often more cynical technocrats—as sentimental nostalgia, a movement that belonged to a world that has passed into history.

Different "in-groups" have emerged, however, in the form of internal lobbies. These lobbies are composed of a few officials with a strong commitment to a specific program. In many cases, they almost might be called "organization men," dedicated to their own particular area of activity and prepared to engage in long, sustained, and persistent efforts to get a specific program through. At the same time, they will push the interests of their own small unit within the bureaucracy, frequently to the exclusion of, and occasionally in conscious and bitter opposition to, the policies advocated by other subunits of the same institution.

Here, the decision-making arena is usually an informal get-together, a small committee meeting, or a strategy session called by the leader of the group. Each tends to correspond to a different type of elite network. The informal get-together is generally the arena for the "old boy" group, the men who have known each other and worked together politically for decades, former Resistance leaders and leaders of the major farm organizations, for example. Highly specialized experts, who come together from the various capitals of the member countries at regular intervals, meet in small committees. Even when the committee is new or an ad hoc creation, its members are usually very quickly socialized into the group. The strategy session is the particular arena of the EEC Commission member or the high-ranking official with his following of loyal staff members.

The process in the elite networks scheme is usually one of subtle, behind-the scenes lobbying and elaborate committee work (often behind closed doors or over dinner, drinks, etc.). Much of the preparatory work takes place over the telephone. There is none of the publicity of the intergovernmental negotiations of the Council of Ministers meeting except in the rare case where an outstanding individual rallies around him a staff of loyal and competent aides. Then the process is highly individual and freewheeling, and it depends a great deal on how the person concerned pursues his cause. It may be through subtle pressures and persuasion of his colleagues. On the other hand, he may engage in a headline-making, public relations speaking campaign.

Behavior patterns vary greatly from one elite network to another, and much depends on the personalities and backgrounds of the men involved. In studying the elite networks, many questions must be asked: How is an individual European official affected by working in close contact with a particularly dynamic EEC Commission member? What loyalties, group feelings, stresses, and tensions emerge when three or four officials over a period of months, often years, plead their case regularly with other units of the same institution, with other institutions and agencies in the same organization, and then, outside, with all the many governments, institutions, and agencies with which they may have to deal? What socializing effects are experienced by the members of an ad hoc committee that meets weekly for several months?

In a provocative survey of integration studies, Ernst Haas points up the importance of knowing

when, how and why actors "learn" to behave differently than they did in the past. Is it a function of cross-national contact and familiarity, as the psychotherapist would have us believe? Is it the result of ever more complex patterns of intergroup loyalties and of social roles that require a single individual to cater to many patterns simultaneously? Is it related to education and informal socialization practices?[9]

Although some research into the dynamics of interpersonal relations in small groups has been conducted by social psychologists, it has not attracted much interest among political scientists. As Philip E. Jacob points out:

Decisions emerging from a group process are found to be strongly affected by the nature of the personalities involved and the way in which the group is organized. . . . For instance, drawing on the observations of small group dynamics, sound policy analysis should take cognizance of the relative rigidity of personality of decision-makers, the patterns of leadership established. . . and the techniques of group management employed.[10]

The elite networks conceptual scheme thus points up the need to examine in detail not just one case study of decision-making but several in order to test the hypothesis that one of the crucial variables in the decision-making process is the personalities of the men involved.

The Case Studies

The five decisions selected for detailed study were:

1. July 1968: abolition of restrictions on the free movement of workers within the European Community;
2. March 1969: conclusion of association agreements between the European Economic Community and Morocco and Tunisia (Rabat and Tunis Agreements);

3. February 1971: proposal for an economic and monetary union between the member countries of the European Community;

4. March 1971: linkage of structural reforms in agriculture to price increases; and

5. June 1971: introduction of generalized preferences on imports from overseas developing countries as of July 1, 1971.

These five decisions were chosen to cover as many variations as possible in time, subject matter, personalities, groups and institutions involved, and external pressures. Provisions for free labor movement were written into the Rome Treaty. Thus, the subject was in the "decisional mill" for ten years and provides a good opportunity to follow variations in decisional processes over time.

Three of the other decisions selected also took many years to receive final approval by the Council of Ministers of the Communities. The Rome Treaty contained provisions, in an annexed declaration of intention, for special agreements with Morocco and Tunisia. Some feelers were in fact put out as early as 1958, but serious overtures were not made until 1963. It took six years to conclude the agreements. During this time, both the European Community and the Maghreb countries went through many political, economic, and social changes, and Morocco and Tunisia radically changed their status on the world scene. This case study therefore should provide valuable insights into the evolution of decision-making processes that involved nonmember countries with special ties (as former dependencies of France) with the Community.

The generalized preferences decision was also chosen because it took a long time to reach fruition. The idea of extending some kind of special preferential advantage to all developing countries was broached in 1963, but this particular measure took two more years than the Maghreb agreements to work out. It was selected, like the Maghreb case, to isolate any special, individual aspects of EEC decision-making in relation to developing countries. It was also selected in order to determine whether there were marked differences between the Community's dealings with countries that had maintained special ties with one of its members, and its dealings with developing countries taken as a broad general group.

The agricultural structures/prices decision was chosen as a contrast to both the Maghreb and the generalized preferences case studies. The agricultural structures decision covered almost the same time span (there was talk of reforming farm structures as early as 1958), but was strictly an internal EEC matter. However, during the 1960s, economic and social conditions in the six member countries of the EEC changed radically. The decade witnessed the institution of the customs union in industrial products between the member states and the introduction of the common agricultural policy with standardized price and marketing conditions for all six countries. The 1960s also saw a massive exodus from the land in many farm regions of the Community. If, in following the proposals to reform farm structures, marked changes in the decision-making approach emerged, then it would be possible to say that the passage of time had some effect on processes. No sharp variations would suggest that time is not one of the crucial variables in the multivariate decision-making process.

In complete contrast with the other four case studies, the decision to introduce an economic and monetary union in the European Community was not provided for in the Rome Treaty, nor was it proposed in as many words until The Hague summit meeting of December 1969. Admittedly, from the early 1960s there had been talk in some Community circles of greater coordination of the economic and monetary policies of the member states, and the launching of the Barre Plan in February 1969 clearly implied a future union. Thus, the decision went through all the essential processes in just fifteen months. It contained provisions intended to cut away drastically at the autonomy of the member states, and yet it went through all the vital processes in near record time. What happened in the Community between 1969 and 1971 to facilitate this speedy approval by the member states? Was it the time factor? the spirit of The Hague summit? or were other considerations, such as people, subject matter, and external pressures more important?

The five case studies were also chosen to illustrate as wide a range as possible of issue areas: social questions; relations with nonmember countries that had for many years maintained special ties with a member country; relations with the developing countries of the third world in the framework of UNCTAD, GATT, and OECD activities; agricultural questions with a long-term impact in their structural reform aspect and short-range effects as far as price changes were concerned; economic and financial changes of short-, medium- and long-term impact and of national, regional, and international importance. By ranging so widely in subject matter, it was posited that differences of approach and behavior in the decision-making processes would validate the hypothesis that processes vary according to the subject under consideration.

Study of the individuals/groups/institutions variable presented problems, since in at least two of the selected cases, the number of different individuals, groups, and institutions involved was very large. This was particularly true for the generalized preferences case. On the other hand, it was decided that such complexity might be fruitful. For example, some light could be shed on the development of leadership roles. Also, the emergence of intra-institutional rivalries as a result of increased bureaucratic specialization could be studied.

Investigation of the generalized preferences decision was considered particularly important in relation to the Maghreb association agreements. Both sets of decisions involved a number of outside organizations, whereas the other was the exclusive preserve of Community institutions. Thus, differences between the two in intrapersonal, intragroup and intrainstitutional interactions could be highly significant.

The free movement of labor decision was likely to provide fertile ground for examining interest group pressures within the Community. Both labor and management were interested in the issue. Also, the subject had been under discussion for many years, in some of its aspect predating the existence of the EEC; the 1951 European Coal and Steel Community Treaty provided for easing labor movements between the member countries. This case, it was thought, might give some indications of how the labor unions and management associations make their voices heard in Brussels.

The agricultural structures/prices decision was also likely to provide important information on interest group pressures, particularly as European level federations of representative agricultural organizations are probably the most vocal of all the many sectoral interest groups active in the European Community. The agricultural structures/prices decision presented two other crucial facets. It provided the only case in European Community history of massive popular demonstrations over a subject of Community concern taking place in Brussels rather than in the national capitals. In other words, it provided the first concrete indication of public awareness that the center of decision-making on some agricultural matters was located in Brussels. Second, the agricultural structures/prices decision provided a superb example of personality and leadership politics, in the person of Sicco Mansholt. Documentary evidence, press reports, and personal interviews all made it very clear that after his appointment to the EEC Commission in 1958, Mr. Mansholt had made an indelible mark on the EEC institutions, on organization leaders in all six Community countries, and on the public at large.

The five case studies also exhibited considerable diversity with respect to external pressures. Much of the preparation for the generalized preferences decision occurred in UNCTAD and, in part, in OECD and GATT. In addition, the ties maintained by the European Community with the eighteen Yaoundé associated African and Malagasy states, which happen also to figure prominently among the group of least developed of the developing countries, added a dimension to the external pressures enquiry. The Community had to decide whether or not to give priority to the eighteen African associates who objected to the disadvantages they could incur if they were put on an equal footing with other developing countries. Finally, throughout the negotiation of the generalized preferences question in UNCTAD, GATT and OECD, the United States long played a role that the EEC viewed as obstructive. This aspect of the negotiations offered some in-teresting insights into EEC-United States relations.

Somewhat similar external pressures apparently entered into play in the Maghreb case. By proposing special trading privileges for Morocco and Tunisia, the Community became involved with most of the other non-member Mediterranean countries, which also asked for special treatment. Since Morocco and Tunisia had Arab world affiliations, the delicate matter of relationships with Israel arose. In the Maghreb case also, the Commu-nity encountered pressure from the United States in GATT, where there were strong American protests against the special trading privileges, par-ticularly for citrus fruit, granted by the Community.

In contrast to these two case studies where the external pressures appeared to be very strong, the free movement of labor decision seemed, in all but one respect, to be relatively free of outside pressures. When immi-grant labor from nonmember countries started to enter the Community in fairly large numbers, significant changes in attitude, particularly among Community labor unions, emerged.

The agricultural structures/prices decision also seemed free of obvious external pressures. However, once it became clear that the Community would in all probability be enlarged to include Great Britain, Norway, Denmark and Ireland, Community leaders in the area started to take projected enlargement effects into account.

The proposed enlargement also played an important part in the process-es leading up to the economic and monetary union decision. By 1969, there was no doubt in anyone's mind that the economies and monetary systems not only of the six member countries of the European Community, but also of all the Western industrialized countries, were intimately connected. The expected inclusion in the Community of Great Britain, with all its attendant monetary, economic, and social problems, could not fail to redirect the course of the decision-making processes.

In addition to the effects of the proposed entry of Great Britain, activity and decisions in the International Monetary Fund and in the Group of Ten of OECD exercised a profound effect on activities and decisions in the European Community. It is quite possible that the speed with which the economic and monetary union decision was reached was due largely to strong pressures from international monetary quarters to engage in wholesale reform of the world monetary system.

An attempt has thus been made to show that, on the basis of four salient variables—time; subject matter; individuals, groups and institutions in-volved; and external pressures exerted—each of the five case studies selected appears to differ from the others in at least one respect and generally in many more. In other words, they differed from each other sufficiently so that an attempt could be made to isolate the factors that influenced the decision-making processes in the different cases and to validate the hypothesis that decision-making processes do indeed vary along several different dimensions. The overlap, however, cannot be ignored. This points to the conclusion that decision-making is not a totally nonrepeatable exercise and that it is possible to make some broad tentative generalizations about the subject.

Analytical Procedures

The analytical procedures followed in the study fell into two main categories: documentary analysis and field interviews. A considerable quantity of official documentary material was available. All the different institutions of the Communities: the Council of Ministers, the EEC Commission and its various directorates general, the European Parliament, and the Economic and Social Committee publish many series of official records. However, serious problems of content were encountered. The official records of the Council of Ministers, the Committee of Permanent Representatives, and the Commission of the EEC and its directorates general usually do not tell us much about who said what, or when, and under what circumstances. The documents of the European Parliament and the Economic and Social Committee are somewhat better in this respect, for both institutions publish minutes of their proceedings.

Official records of the interest groups appear to be almost nonexistent. A good number of the larger interest groups, particularly Community federations of national groups with headquarters in Brussels, publish reasonably informative press releases containing statements of opinion on issues of particular concern to them. It is thus often possible to locate anxiety and pinpoint the times when it was expressed. One particularly invaluable source of information, not only on opinions expressed by the pressure groups, but also in the national parliaments and at diverse meetings of European Community interest, was found to be the quarterly *Survey of European Documentation*, published by the general directorate of parliamentary documentation and information of the secretariat of the European Parliament.

Even this highly informative and wide-ranging source of material did not give any pointers to prevailing moods and emotions. Were comments defensive or conciliatory, angry or amiable? The only available indications of expressed emotions were obtained from the press. The general daily press was some help, particularly the wide range of detailed articles on Community affairs that regularly appear in *Le Monde*. The daily bulletins published by the specialized news agency commonly known as *Agence*

Europe were drawn upon with the greatest frequency and proved to be of enormous value. *Agence Europe* is almost a watchword in every European Community office and in every organization that has dealings with the EEC. It is universally recognized as reliable and is frequently cited by officials even before the piece of information in question has been widely disseminated.

The material obtained from the documentary evidence was considerably fleshed out by field work in Brussels, Luxembourg, and Strasbourg. With the exception of some semirestricted memoranda, letters, etc., all the evidence obtained in the field came from interviews. It should be pointed out at this juncture that I worked for five years as an information specialist in one of the regional offices of the press and information service of the European Communities. In that capacity, I met many Community officials, and this provided an invaluable starting point for the interviews. A totally open-ended interviewing style was adopted. Whenever possible, officials were selected who were already known personally to the author or to whom the author had been personally recommended. On most occasions, therefore, a relationship of confidence was established fairly quickly.

No set questionnaire was used, as an attempt was made to get at the motivations and emotions involved in the various stages of the decision-making. The interviewer assiduously discouraged officials from recounting "the facts of the case" and encouraged them as much as possible to reminisce, tell anecdotes, even joke about their own and their colleagues' roles. With very few exceptions this technique seemed to come almost as a relief to officials who, over time, have grown accustomed to answering detailed, technical questionnaires geared to current fashions in the American political science community rather than to enquiring about people and events. Some of the most productive interviews were obtained in analytically unorthodox, unbusinesslike surroundings: perched on a low wall surrounding flowerbeds in front of the EEC Commission headquarters; in the luncheonette frequented by those members of the Commission staff who work under severe pressures and who do not have the time for leisurely lunch appointments; driving through the Lorraine countryside from Luxembourg to a plenary session of the European Parliament in Strasbourg with a high-ranking secretariat member—a captive subject *par excellence*!

Although field research in the capitals of the member states other than Brussels and Luxembourg was not possible, an attempt was made to fill in this gap by interviewing officials from the permanent delegations of the member states to the European Communities in Brussels. On a number of occasions these officials were extremely cooperative and made arrangements to be interviewed at times when visiting experts from the national capitals were present. Clearly, however, a much richer picture would have been obtained had interviewing been possible in Paris, Rome, Bonn, and The Hague.

A second caveat: in two of the case studies, the agricultural structures/prices decision and the economic and monetary union case, the interviews were conducted at a time (the first months of 1972) when intensive negotiation was taking place on the implementing legislation. It was not easy to induce officials to cast their minds back a year or more to negotiations on a subject very closely related to the one foremost in their minds at the time of the interviews. This was particularly true for economic and monetary officials who had to circumvent an official embargo on outside interviews.

The interviews conducted in the field crystallized and confirmed an idea that had been in my mind during five years as a participant observer: it is the men who govern the processes and not the processes that govern the men. In other words, although time, subject matter, external pressures, and personalities are all extremely important variables, the last carries the greatest weight. It was the elite networks conceptual scheme that seemed to throw most light on the course of decision-making processes in the European Community. In all the case studies, elite networks tended to emerge both in intergovernmental politics and where grass-roots pressures were exerted. As Robert Russell pointed out in his preliminary study of international monetary elites:

The small group model . . . stresses the potential for the group process itself to lead to outcomes . . . which are not a simple combination of aims, resources, and actions of abstract national actors. . . . The group would show a tendency to carry on activity based upon its own dynamic character and that of the individual participants.[11]

Thus, the overlap of intrapersonal relations became extremely important, for it provided the link between the three conceptual schemes.

With the exception of chapter 2, which provides an historical account of the main negotiating steps in each of the case studies, each of the following chapters deals with one case study viewed in turn through the three conceptual lenses: the intergovernmental politics lens, the grass-roots lens, and the elite network lens. Finally, the concluding chapter attempts to make some generalizations about decision-making in the EEC and to elaborate on the small-group dynamics link among the three separate approaches.

2 The Five Decisions: The Case Histories

The Introduction of Generalized Preferences

On June 22, 1971, the Council of Ministers of the European Community decided that the EEC would give generalized tariff preferences to imports from developing countries as of July 1.

In 1958, a report drawn up for the General Agreement on Tariffs and Trade (GATT) by a group of experts suggested that developed countries should refrain from protecting their industries against imports of manufactured goods from developing countries. This idea was pioneered in GATT by a number of developing countries, led by India. In 1963, in GATT, the EEC member countries and the states associated with the Community suggested that "one of the appropriate measures to be discussed rapidly [with a view to promoting the developing countries' trade and their development] would be to grant preferential treatment to semi-finished goods and manufactures exported by the developing countries."[1]

At the first session of the United Nations Conference on Trade and Development (UNCTAD) held in Geneva in mid-1964, the majority of the states represented, including the EEC member countries, agreed in principle that the industrialized countries should grant such preferences. The Final Act of the Conference, adopted on June 15, 1964, contained the following declaration, otherwise known as the Eighth "General Principle":

Recognizing the urgent need for the diversification and expansion of the export trade of developing countries in manufactures and semi-manufactures in order to narrow as rapidly as possible the commercial deficit resulting from present trends in international trade. . . .

Noting that all the developing countries and a great majority of the developed countries have signified their agreement with the principle of assisting the industrial development of developing countries by the extension of preferences in their favour. . . .

Noting that a programme of work on the question has been agreed upon in the General Agreement on Tariffs and Trade, and that the Contracting Parties have affirmed their intention to go ahead with it,

Recommends that the Secretary-General of the United Nations make appropriate arrangements for the establishment as soon as possible of a committee of governmental representatives drawn both from developed and developing countries to consider the matter with a view to working out the best method of implementing such preferences on the basis of non-reciprocity from the developing countries.[2]

15

Several steps toward implementing the General Principle were taken in 1965. The new Part Four of the GATT Agreement departed from the principle of reciprocity by stipulating: "The developed contracting parties do not expect reciprocity for commitments entered into by them in trade negotiations to reduce or eliminate tariffs and other barriers to the trade of undeveloped contracting parties."[3] In the United Nations in May 1965 the secretary-general set up a special committee to deal with the subject. The Organization for Economic Cooperation and Development (OECD) also set up a special group, the so-called Group of Four, with representatives of the United States, Great Britain, Germany, and France, to study proposals from the industrial countries.

To enable the EEC Council of Ministers to agree on a Community attitude on generalized preferences and, as part of the preparation for a Community position at the Second United Nations Conference on Trade and Development (UNCTAD II), in November 1966 the EEC Commission forwarded a memorandum to the Council. It reaffirmed clearly that the Community was in favor of the principle of granting preferences, but on a product-by-product, not an automatic, basis.[4]

The developing countries also made preparations for UNCTAD II. Meeting in Algiers in October 1967, the ministers of the "Group of 77" agreed on a series of unanimous recommendations, to be known as the "Charter of Algiers." Under the heading "Principles of a General System of Preferences," the charter stated:

At the second conference negotiations should be held with a view to concluding an agreement on a general system of tariff preferences on a nondiscriminatory basis. This agreement should provide for free entry, without restrictions of any kind, of all manufactures and semimanufactures of developing countries to the markets of all industrial countries.[5]

In addition, the OECD Group of Four completed its report and submitted it to the OECD Council late in November 1967. The ministers agreed that the Group's study should be used as a joint platform for the delegations of the member governments at UNCTAD II and in future discussions of this matter.

UNCTAD II, held in New Delhi in February and March 1968, marked the second stage in the process of establishing generalized preferences for the developing countries. The New Delhi meeting provided the opportunity for a wide exchange of views on the basis of the preparatory work carried out by the various groups. It culminated in the adoption of Resolution 21 (II) which recognized that unanimous agreement had been reached on the "early establishment of a mutually acceptable system of generalized non-reciprocal and non-discriminatory preferences which would be beneficial to the developing countries."[6]

The task of settling remaining problems was entrusted to the UNCTAD Special Committee on Preferences. It began to draw up a work program to allow UNCTAD to meet the December 31, 1969 deadline set in New Delhi for completing work on generalized preferences. Also in implementation of Resolution 21 (II), in OECD, where the Western countries had been coordinating their positions on the subject, a special ad hoc working party was set up. It was composed of those industrialized countries that intended to grant generalized preferences to the developing countries. The EEC Commission took an active part in this working party. It was agreed that any country intending to grant preferences should deposit two lists of products with OECD by March 1, 1969. For manufactures and semimanufactures, each donor country would make a list of products to be excluded from the general preferences it was prepared to grant. For processed agricultural products, the donors would list products that might receive preferential treatment.

The EEC Council of Ministers was able to deposit a list of manufactures and semimanufactures with OECD on schedule in early March 1969, and at the end of October of the same year, the Council of Ministers decided to transmit these preliminary offers as they stood to UNCTAD. The offers were based on the assumption that the main industrialized OECD countries would participate in the preferences and make comparable concessions.

Intensive consultations were held throughout most of 1970 at the Community level, in the UNCTAD Special Committee on Preferences, and in OECD in an attempt to get the system of generalized preferences off the ground at the earliest possible opportunity. In October the UNCTAD Special Committee was able to submit its report to the UNCTAD Trade Board. This paved the way for the EEC Council of Ministers to decide at the end of March 1971 to set July 1, 1971 as the target date for implementation of generalized tariff preferences by the European Community. Finally, at its June 21-22 session, the Council adopted a whole series of regulations and decisions to be applied for a six-month period as of July 1, 1971: six regulations dealing with manufactured and semimanufactured products, one regulation concerning processed agricultural products, and two decisions concerning products coming under the Coal and Steel Community treaty.

The countries of the European Community were thus the first to introduce generalized preferences on imports from developing countries. The decision, according to EEC Commission President Malfatti, was the most important international step that the Community had taken since the conclusion of the Kennedy Round. The action, he said, was only the beginning of a more active policy for dealing with the problems of world development.[7]

The Association Agreements with Morocco and Tunisia

When the Treaty of Rome was signed in March 1957, the six member states of the European Community declared their readiness to propose to the independent countries of the franc area "the opening of negotiations with a view to concluding conventions for economic association with the Community."[8] The Tunisian government started to put out feelers on the subject as early as 1959 and, on a number of later occasions, expressed a desire to follow up on the Rome Treaty provisions. However, no concrete steps were taken either by Tunisia or Morocco at that time, since it was felt that the Algerian situation should be settled first. Algerian independence in mid-1962 opened up the way to a shift in policy. In October 1963, Tunisia and, in December, Morocco submitted applications to Brussels for the opening of negotiations.[9]

Exploratory talks took place in 1964. Tunisia and Morocco asked for the widest possible preferential arrangements within a free trade area. They also urged that allowances should be made for the less-developed state of their economies. In addition, they sought financial aid, technical assistance, and freer movement of their workers to the Community. Actual negotiations, begun in July 1965, made little progress, largely because of the severe limitations placed by the Community Council of Ministers on the EEC Commission, the negotiating body for the Europeans. The Commission's negotiating mandate was restricted to commercial issues. Moreover, it did not cover a number of export products important for the Maghreb countries.

Largely because of political difficulties within the Community, the EEC Commission was not given broader negotiating power until October 1967. When negotiations resumed in November 1967 on the basis of a broadened Commission mandate, the Maghreb countries asked for a rapid conclusion of agreements, with immediate applicability even if the arrangements were limited. However, a guarantee was obtained that the partial association envisaged would be only a first step toward comprehensive association agreements. The two agreements that emerged after a further ten months of discussion were limited to trade and contained no provisions for financial aid, technical assistance, or free movement of labor.

The Rabat and Tunis Agreements, although strictly commercial, are based on Article 238 of the Rome Treaty, which states that agreements may be concluded "creating an association embodying reciprocal rights and obligations, joint actions and special procedures."[10] Even though the agreements by no means exhausted the full potential of the 1957 Declaration of Intention, they constituted quite an important step toward its full application. Under the commercial arrangements, free trade areas were established between the European Community and Tunisia and between the Community and Morocco. All industrial products, except cork and iron and steel products, would enter the Common Market duty free and without quantitative restrictions. Special provisions were included for petroleum products and processed foodstuffs. For agricultural products the concessions offered by the European Community varied, but were largely designed to maintain the protection and preferences enjoyed by Community producers while at the same time preserving the existing balance between competing Mediterranean producers. The special advantages that exports of the two associated countries enjoyed in the French market (duty-free entry for specific quantities of products) also had to be taken into account. Morocco was granted an important preference on citrus fruit and Tunisia on crude olive oil.

In return for these trade benefits, Tunisia accorded a special preferential tariff to the member countries of the EEC to be introduced over a thirty-six-month period. Morocco, prevented by the 1906 Act of Algeçiras from granting preferences, could not give the Community members any such privileges (this situation had also applied in Morocco's trade relationships with France prior to the signature of the association agreement), but it did make some fairly substantial concessions with respect to quantitative restrictions.

The two association agreements contained a number of procedural and institutional innovations. Most important, they provided for the opening after three years of new negotiations for more comprehensive terms of association. The Six thus gave assurances, but no binding commitments, that they would offer some noncommercial concessions after three years, as well as filling in certain gaps in the commercial arrangements.

Also, the Community broke with the tradition followed in all the previous association agreements (with the African and Malagasy States; Greece; Turkey; Nigeria; and Kenya, Uganda and Tanzania) in which the governments of the six member states participate alongside the Council of Ministers. In this case the sole contracting party to the agreements on the Community side was the Council of Ministers. As a corollary to this break with tradition, the Maghreb association agreements also omitted the requirement written into other association agreements for separate parliamentary ratification. The Rabat and Tunis Agreements were thus the first association agreements to go into effect without lengthy and difficult parliamentary ratification in the six member states. The association agreement signed with Nigeria, on July 16, 1966, for example, expired before it had been ratified by all the contracting parties. The first Arusha Agreement signed with Kenya, Uganda, and Tanzania on July 26, 1968 expired on May 31, 1969, before it had been ratified. The second agreement, which was signed on September 24, 1969, was not fully ratified until the end of December 1970.

The negotiation and conclusion of the Maghreb association agreements set in motion a series of "domino effect" demands from other countries in the area. They also provoked a series of protests from the United States in GATT that the EEC was starting up a network of expansionist preferential trading arrangements. Thus, both directly and indirectly, the two Maghreb association agreements had far-reaching implications.

Free Movement of Labor Within the Community

The concept of free movement of labor between the Six was first introduced under the European Coal and Steel Community Treaty of April 1951. Article 69 of the ECSC treaty specified that if any one member country had a shortage of skilled labor, available labor from the other member countries would be permitted to take the vacant jobs.[11]

The treaty establishing the European Economic Community greatly extended the ECSC provisions for the free movement of labor. Article 48 provided for "the abolition of any discrimination based on nationality between workers of the Member States as regards employment, remuneration, and other working conditions."[12] Article 49 set out the procedures for the gradual implementation of the provisions of Article 48. For this purpose, the Council of Ministers was to issue, on the basis of a proposal from the Commission, the necessary directives and regulations. Article 148, paragraph 1 governed the procedural questions of a simple majority which applies in this case. The Economic and Social Committee must be consulted. Consultation of the European Parliament is, however, optional. Article 49 provided four main methods by which the free movement of workers was to be achieved:

(a) by ensuring close collaboration between national labour administrations;

(b) by progressively abolishing according to a plan any such administrative procedures and practices and also any such time limits in respect of eligibility for available employment . . . the maintenance of which would be an obstacle to the freeing of the movement of workers;

(c) by progressively abolishing according to a plan all such time limits and other restrictions . . . as impose on workers of other Member States conditions for the free choice of employment different from those imposed on workers of the State concerned; and

(d) by setting up appropriate administrative machinery for connecting offers of employment and requests for employment, with a view to equilibrating them in such a way as to avoid serious threats to the standard of living and employment in the various regions and industries.

In August 1961, the first EEC measures providing for the free movement of labor were issued, to go into effect as of September 1, 1961 (EEC Regulation No. 15). Proposals for these measures had been made by the EEC Commission in June 1960; the Economic and Social Committee had been consulted, and the European Parliament had issued an opinion.

Under Regulation No. 15, workers had to have specific job offers before they could move to another country. The member states designated official employment agencies whose work was coordinated by the EEC Commission. In addition, a tripartite consultative committee (representatives of labor, management, and the six governments) was established to advise the Commission on policies affecting the free movement of labor.[13]

In 1962, the European Economic Community entered into the second of the three stages provided for in the Rome Treaty in the transition to a fully integrated economy. In October 1962, the Commission sent to the Council of Ministers a new draft regulation and directives that provided for much greater labor mobility. The Council of Ministers, after obtaining the opinion of the European Parliament and the Economic and Social Committee, approved the new regulation and its accompanying directives in March 1964, and it went into effect on May 1 of that year as Regulation No. 38, superceding Regulation No. 15.

The new regulation, unlike Regulation No. 15, covered frontier and seasonal labor, not just permanent workers. It also dropped the earlier provision giving national labor markets priority, although exceptional rules could be made to prevent imbalances on the labor market in any given region or occupation. Under the 1964 regulation, a foreign worker who had been employed regularly for two years in a Community country was permitted to engage in any wage-earning occupation in that country. He thus acquired the same right to change jobs as a national of that country. Under the earlier regulation, four years of prior employment had been necessary.

Foreign workers acquired rights to belong to labor unions. They became eligible for election as officers of unions subject to the laws of the individual state regulating collective bargaining. A worker had to be resident for at least three years in the member country where he was employed to be eligible for election, although he could become a union member when he accepted a job. Progress was also made on allowing workers, to be joined by their families. The 1961 regulation had imposed rather strict limitations in this area. As of May 1, 1964, workers could be joined by close relatives and other family members so long as they could provide reasonable living accommodations for them.[14]

In May 1966 the EEC Council of Ministers reached an agreement on a target date of July 1, 1968 (eighteen months ahead of the date originally scheduled) for the elimination of all restrictions on the movement of industrial and agricultural goods between the member states of the European Community. There was then a call for introducing free movement of labor by the same date. With this in view, the EEC Commission submitted proposals for a regulation and a directive to the Council of Ministers on April 7, 1967. The Council then consulted the European Parliament and the Economic and Social Committee. The European Parliament gave a favorable opinion on the proposals in mid-October, and at the end of the month, the Economic and Social Committee also rendered a favorable opinion. Early in 1968, on the basis of the reactions of the two bodies, the Commission submitted revised proposals to the Council. Finally, on July 29, 1968, the Council of Ministers adopted this last in the series of regulations, No. 1612, and its accompanying directives.

Regulation No. 1612 abandoned the concept of "national priority" and gave nationals of other member states the same access to employment as nationals. It abolished work permits so that EEC workers could take jobs without having to comply with any formalities except those required for residence permits, and it extended the right to apply for a job to workers of any member state. Non-nationals were also given a whole series of rights that insured the same treatment as national workers: membership in labor unions; the same tax treatment and social benefits; the right to be joined by members of their families and dependents in their new residence; access to living accommodations and property on the same conditions as nationals. The new regulation also confirmed an important principle, "Community priority." In other words, Community workers occupied a privileged position over workers from nonmember countries. A series of provisions was also made to improve the exchange of information on job vacancies in member countries. Finally, the new regulation allowed for action in the event of "serious threats to the standard of living and employment" in any given region, although, in contrast to the situation under the earlier regulations, regulatory measures of that nature could no longer be decreed unilaterally but had to be processed through Community channels.[15] Thus, in exactly ten years, the European Community fully implemented, on paper at any rate, the provisions of the Rome Treaty eighteen months ahead of schedule.

Agricultural Prices and Structures

Article 39, paragraph 1 of the Rome Treaty specifies that a major aim of the common agricultural policy in the European Community should be an increase in the individual earnings of persons engaged in agriculture, thereby ensuring them a fair standard of living.[16] It had been universally recognized that agriculture was lagging behind other economic sectors, with lower productivity, incomes, and living standards. From the outset, Community experts asserted that the aims of the common agricultural policy could not be fully realized through market and price policies alone, and proposals to improve agricultural structures were put forward from the first years of the Community's existence.

"Agricultural structure," according to the EEC Commission, means:

the whole body of production and living conditions in the agriculture of a given region. This structure sets a limit to the possibilities of combining the factors of production and of organizing the farm, and it determines the living conditions of the population. Consequently, the structure of agriculture is one of the factors which determine the level of productivity that is attainable in a given market and price situation, the incomes and—to a great extent—the social conditions of those engaged in agriculture.[17]

In its first major memorandum on agriculture, the so-called Green Bible of 1960, the EEC Commission proposed a comprehensive policy covering not only pricing and market organization but also structural reform. However, whereas unified price and market policies were envisaged, coordination only among the member states was projected for structures. In November 1960, the Council of Ministers issued the following statement:

Action must be taken to co-ordinate and encourage the measures by which the Member States seek to improve the structure of agriculture; the necessity for such action stems in part from the way in which structural and market policies affect each other, in part from the need to seize every opportunity to increase the economic strength and the competitiveness of agriculture.[18]

In accordance with these general statements of principle and in order to increase cooperation between the member states and the EEC Commission, the EEC Council of Ministers, on December 4, 1962, issued a decision creating a Standing Committee on Agricultural Structures, to be attached to the Commission and composed of representatives of the member states. It was to be presided over by a member of the Commission. The committee was to examine national structural policies, and the connection between these and regional development and agricultural markets policies. The committee was also required to assist the Commission in the preparation of an annual report to be submitted by the Commission to the European Parliament and the Council of Ministers. The report would consist of a survey of the member states' agricultural structures and policies, measures taken and their effectiveness, and information on the coordination of agricultural structures at the Community level. On the basis of these annual reports, the Council would adopt the measures needed to coordinate the member states' policies on agricultural structures. The member states were also required to communicate to the Commission projects for new laws and regulations, long-range plans, and regional programs that included measures for improving structures. The Commission could express its opinion on these projects.[19]

Although the provisions of the December 1962 decision were fairly wide-reaching, they were not deemed sufficient to enable the EEC Commission to promote structural improvements, especially measures involving the Community as a whole. Consequently, in March 1963 the Commission submitted a proposal to the Council for the establishment of a European Fund for Structural Improvements in Agriculture.[20] The proposed fund, however, never came into being, and no great progress was made toward improving agricultural structures for several years. With the exception of some activity in the Standing Committee, little happened until the autumn of 1967.

As the barriers that divided the markets of the six member countries were gradually abolished for a wide range of agricultural products, intra-Community trade increased markedly. Prices of the main agricultural products were fixed by Community institutions entrusted with the management of markets. The Community prepared to assume financial responsibility for its agricultural policy and to introduce Community arrangements for trade in agricultural products with nonmember countries. All these factors threw into high relief the increasing discrepancy between farm incomes and those of other social and occupational groups. It was maintained, particularly in EEC Commission circles, that new, bold structures and a long-term view were needed. It was considered essential to have production and marketing structures that would enable farmers to enjoy all the advantages of the single Community market. In accordance with a Council request made in October 1967, the EEC Commission embarked on a thorough analysis of the situation.

"Agriculture 1980," a Commission memorandum on the reform of Community agriculture, was submitted to the Council of Ministers on December 10, 1968. The plan was in fact a dossier of several closely linked documents dealing with the reform of agriculture in the six member countries of the Community over a ten-year period. The key document in the dossier was the "Memorandum on the Reform of Agriculture in the European Economic Community." This was accompanied by two others: "Medium-term Measures for Various Agricultural Markets" and "Commission Proposals to the Council on the Fixing of Prices for Certain Agricultural Products for 1969/70." The dossier was completed by a "Report on the Situation of Agriculture and the Agricultural Markets" and a "Report Concerning Policies on the Structure of Agriculture Followed by Community Countries."

The plan, drafted under the aegis of the Commission's vice-president, Sicco Mansholt (from whom it acquired the name "Mansholt Plan"), was designed to eliminate discrepancies between rural and urban standards of living. Small, inefficient farms were to be consolidated into large production units. Two million of the Community's ten million farmers were to be retired or trained for other occupations. Balance between supply and demand for agricultural commodities was to be improved. The cost of the program was to be shared equally by the European Agricultural Guidance and Guarantee Fund and the individual member countries involved in the project.[21]

The suggestions and ideas outlined in the memorandum, which had implications far beyond the sphere of agriculture proper, were widely discussed in all quarters. The Council of Ministers, following a preliminary discussion in December 1968, in May 1969 gave the Special Committee on Agriculture the task of examining the structural measures proposed in the memorandum. The Special Committee, in its turn, set up an ad hoc working party to prepare a report on the technical agricultural problems raised by the Commission's proposals. The European Parliament asked five of its committees to examine the memorandum: the Committee on Agriculture, the Legal Affairs Committee, the Economic Affairs Committee, the Committee on Social Affairs and Health Protection, and the Committee for Finance and Budgets. The Economic and Social Committee set up a special ad hoc subcommittee to prepare a report on the memorandum, and it worked for almost a year before submitting it to the plenary session of the Committee in late November of 1969.

As a sequel to its December 1968 memorandum, the EEC Commission submitted a further set of proposals to the Council at the end of April 1970—the "Mini-Mansholt Plan." The draft legislation took up, in somewhat modified form, most of the ideas of the 1968 memorandum: to create viable modern farms run by well-trained farmers receiving an adequate income; to protect farmers who leave the land to retire or to learn a new trade; to convert farmland into forests and parks; to switch production from surplus commodities (wheat, sugar, and dairy products) to shortage commodities (beef and veal); to increase the responsibility of farmers for marketing their own produce. The new plan covered only the period until 1975 rather than 1980.[22]

Almost another full year went by, however, before the Council of Ministers reached any substantive decision on agricultural structures. In February 1971 the EEC Commission issued the member countries with an ultimatum: any country that wanted price increases for its farm products must also support reform of the basic structure of farming. At two March sessions, culminating in a marathon session from March 22 to March 25, the Council of Ministers finally agreed to the Commission's "Memorandum and Draft Council Resolution Concerning the New Guidelines of the Common Agricultural Policy."[23]

The Commission's package of proposals provided for somewhat higher prices for agricultural commodities but for less expensive, less ambitious measures in the structural and social fields. It was agreed that the provisions for structural reform would be valid for four years and would be financed by guidance funds already allocated within the common farm fund. The Commission proposed that the common farm fund finance 25 percent of the cost of structural reform projects. In backward areas, however, it was to contribute 65 percent of the total eligible cost.

It was hoped that in the long run a major shift in emphasis in the common agricultural policy toward structural reform could end overproduction by marginal producers, lead to a more prosperous farming community, lower the burden resulting from price support and export subsidies on the Community taxpayer, and ease relations with large agricultural exporters.[24]

Economic and Monetary Union by the End of the 1970s

On February 9, 1971, the Council of Ministers of the European Communities designated the end of the 1970s as the period by which an economic and monetary union should be established between the member states. This decision, like several of those discussed above, can be traced back to the Rome Treaty and the beginnings of the EEC.

The treaty establishing the European Economic Community is based on the principle that economic, cyclical, and monetary policies come under the authority of the member states. However, it was considered necessary to coordinate national policies in these areas and for the member states to consider general Community interests when they adopted economic and monetary measures.[25] In order to coordinate national economic and monetary policies, the Rome Treaty provided for a series of consultative agencies between the member states and the central banks.[26] But the procedures introduced tended to be slow, cumbersome and, in the event of serious economic or financial disturbances, inadequate.

In order to fill the gaps on economic and monetary questions in the Rome Treaty, as early as March 1960 the Council of Ministers issued a decision to improve coordination of member states' short-term economic policies. In October 1962 the EEC Commission took a big step forward when it issued "The Action Programme of the Community for the Second Stage," a memorandum that outlined its ideas for the next stage in the establishment of the common market. Two chapters in the memorandum were devoted to economic and monetary policies. The economic policy chapter defined short-term objectives and discussed goals looking ahead to 1968. In the monetary field, the Commission proposed that from the end of the transitional period, if not even sooner, there should be fixed rates of exchange between the member states with very narrow limits on the variations allowed. By the end of the third stage, the Commission suggested, a full monetary union could be envisaged.

As promised in the Action Programme, the EEC Commission addressed recommendations to the Council of Ministers in June 1963 that were designed to strengthen existing monetary cooperation in the Community meetings of minsters of finance, the Monetary Committee, and the Short-Term Economic Policy Committee. The recommendations were aimed at creating serviceable institutions for monetary cooperation and laying down procedures for consultation prior to any important monetary decisions. The Commission's recommendations were embodied in a series of decisions and declarations issued by the Council of Ministers on May 8, 1964. Provision was made for setting up a committee of governors of central banks. Also, a budget policy committee, composed of senior officials from the ministries of finance of the six member states and of representatives from the EEC Commission, was established. In international monetary affairs, the member states pledged themselves to consult each other before making any change in exchange rates and agreed to hold discussions in the Monetary Committee before taking steps connected with the general working of the international monetary system, having recourse to funds available under international agreements or participating in large-scale support arrangements on behalf of nonmember countries.

In September 1964 the EEC Commission issued another major policy statement along the lines of the 1962 Action Programme. "Initiative 1964" was contained in a memorandum to the Council of Ministers and the governments of the member states and urged increased economic, social, and political integration. The section on monetary policy reads:

The Commission considers that the aims set out in its Action Programme of October 1962 have become even more pressing and that they should be examined in the light of experience. The interpenetration of markets which has meanwhile come about between the Member States makes progress in the field of monetary policy increasingly urgent.

The aim of the Community is not merely to expand trade between the Member States; it implies merging the six markets in a single internal market and the establishment of an economic union. It therefore appears indispensable to adapt the monetary policy of the Six to the degree of integration already attained in other fields.

The Commission will submit without delay to the Council proposals for the progressive introduction of a monetary union.[27]

Despite the Action Programme, the May 1964 decisions, and "Initiative 1964," the only concrete measures taken until late 1968 to implement the various policy statements were the adoption in April 1967 of the Community's first medium-term economic policy program, which covered the years 1966-67 and its completion in 1968 by a second program. However, these two programs contributed little to advancing the coordination of economic policies or avoiding monetary crises. Considerable criticism was directed at this lack of progress by various Community bodies, particularly the European Parliament. The EEC Commission, in its tenth annual report, also pointed to the problems:

Co-ordination of policies has run into the same obstacles as in previous years. The action taken by the various committees concerned in this work has brought imbalances to light and has made it possible to establish what remedial action should be taken. But although the confrontation of national policies at Community level seems to have led to a start being made with co-ordination, it has not ensured that it is carried through with the necessary speed and efficacy.[28]

By 1968 it was very clear that the economies of the member countries were becoming increasingly sensitive to external stimuli. Also, the range and effectiveness of the instruments that could be brought to bear to preserve a balance were steadily declining. The urgency of the situation was underscored by the French political crisis of May 1968. Growing economic and monetary insecurity had to be offset by stronger Community policies. Consequently, on December 5, 1968, the EEC Commission submitted to the Council of Ministers a memorandum "on appropriate policy in the Community on current economic and monetary problems." It also announced that it would propose the setting up of monetary cooperation machinery within the Community to the Council before February 15, 1969. Discussion of the Commission memorandum in the Council on December 12, 1968 showed that there was a broad measure of agreement on the need for greater convergence of economic policies and for intensifying monetary cooperation.[29]

The "Commission Memorandum to the Council on the Co-ordination of Economic Policies and Monetary Co-operation Within the Community" of February 12, 1969, otherwise known as the Barre Plan, emerged out of the December discussions. The Commission, in line with the policy it had defined and advocated for several years, made three broad recommendations: convergence of national medium-term economic policy lines, closer coordination of short-term economic policies, and establishment of Community machinery for monetary cooperation through short-term arrangements for monetary support and possibilities for medium-term financial assistance.[30]

After reiteration of these concerns on a number of occasions during the first half of 1969, the positive result of the Barre Plan was the July 17 Council decision on coordinating member states' short-term economic policies. Confirmation of the need to introduce a real economic and monetary union came at the end of the year at The Hague summit conference.

The heads of state or government, in their December 2 final communiqué, reaffirmed

their will to press forward with the further developments needed if the Community is to be strengthened and its development into an economic union promoted. They are of the opinion that the integration process should result in a Community of stability and growth. To this end they agreed within the Council, on the basis of the memorandum presented by the Commission on 12 February 1969, and in close collaboration with the Commission, a plan in stages should be worked out during 1970 with a view to the creation of an economic and monetary union.

The development of monetary co-operation should be backed up by the harmonization of economic policies.[31]

The Hague recommendations were the prelude to three months of quite vigorous Community activity on economic and monetary matters. At its March 6, 1970 session, the Council of Ministers decided

to invite the chairmen of the Monetary Committee, the Committee of Governors of Central Banks, the Medium-term Economic Policy Committee, the Short-term Economic Policy Committee, and the Budget Policy Committee, as well as a Commission representative, to meet under the chairmanship of M. Pierre Werner and draw up a report comprising an analysis of the various suggestions and enabling the fundamental choices to be made for a phased establishment of the economic and monetary union of the Community.[32]

The Werner Committee, as this Council-sponsored committee became known, began work at the end of March on drafting the report called for in the Council's decision. It was able to get an interim report out by the end of May and to submit a final report to the Commission and the Council at the beginning of October 1970. The report sought to develop a coherent view of all the problems and to make detailed suggestions, in particular for the first stage. On many points the principles adopted by the Commission in its March memorandum were adopted.

At the end of October, the Commission, after studying the Werner Report, forwarded a memorandum to the Council in which it expressed its views on the Committee's findings. The memorandum was accompanied by three documents: a draft resolution, a proposal for a Council decision on the strengthening of the coordination of the member states' short-term policies, and a draft Council decision on increased cooperation between the central banks of the Six. During November and December 1970 and January 1971, the problems of establishing the economic and monetary union by stages were discussed in detail by the Council, the Commission, the European Parliament, and the Economic and Social Committee.

On February 9, 1971, the Council of Ministers of the European Community adopted the following resolution (subsequently formalized on March 22):

In order to assure satisfactory growth, full employment and internal stability of the Community; in order to remedy structural and regional imbalances in evidence; in order to strengthen the contribution of the Community to international economic and monetary cooperation and thus to arrive at a stable and growing Community, the Council and the representatives of member states express their political will to establish over the next ten years an economic and monetary union according to a plan by stages, beginning January 1, 1971.[33]

A series of objectives was set for 1980. People, goods, services, and capital were to circulate freely in the Community without adverse competitive or regional effects. A unified monetary apparatus was to be established, characterized by complete and irreversible convertibility of currencies, elimination of fluctuation margins, and the establishment of parity as prerequisites to a single currency and formation of a Community organization of central banks. Institutions empowered to execute Community policy decisions would also be set up.[34]

The European Community, therefore, by its economic and monetary union decision made a giant step forward on the road to integrating an area that had always been considered the preserve of the member states. Although the decision required an enormous amount of implementing legislation, it broke much new ground in the unification of governmental processes in the six member states.

3

Generalized Preferences

The generalized preferences decision was initially chosen as a case study because it appeared to be an almost pure case of intergovernmental decision-making politics (Conceptual Scheme I.) Although the final decision to introduce tariff preferences to all overseas developing countries was taken by the European Community unilaterally, most of the preparatory work and discussion took place within the framework of international organizations, OECD and UNCTAD in particular. However, when the decision is observed through each of the other two conceptual lenses, two additional dimensions emerge. In the first place, from an early stage in the discussions there were strong grass-roots pressures at work within the Community fighting the whole idea of generalized preferences, particularly by the representative organizations of a number of processing industries. In the second place, from the very outset, extremely strong pressures in favor of generalized preferences were exerted by a small group of officials from within the EEC Commission's directorate general for external affairs (D.G. I.) The case study thus presents an interesting pattern of cross pressures during a seven-year period. It also provides an excellent opportunity to measure the relative strength of the various pressures at work at different times.

Image I: The Governments Dispute the Methods

When the idea of generalized preferences was first broached in GATT in 1963 and then taken up in Geneva at UNCTAD I in the following year, the member states of the European Community all agreed that the industrial countries should give some special form of aid to the developing countries in order to help expand their exports. Beyond this point, however, the member states of the Community dropped their united front and adopted quite different stands on the desired methods.

These differences were accentuated by the Community's very awkward procedural situation at UNCTAD I. The EEC's status at the first United Nations Conference on Trade and Development was that of observer. As such it had the right to speak but not to vote. Normally, therefore, it would be represented by a delegation composed of both Council of Ministers and EEC Commission officials. However, the Council could have requested the EEC Commission to represent the Community at the meetings.[1] This it did not do, and as a result, a curiously ambivalent and complicated situation emerged. All six member states of the Community sent national representatives to the Conference. The representatives each spoke for their own states and voted on an individual basis. Since Belgium was presiding over the Council of Ministers during the first half of 1964, Mr. Maurice Brasseur, the Belgian minister of foreign trade and technical assistance, addressed the Conference in behalf of the Community on March 24, 1964. In addition, Mr. Jean Rey, a member of the EEC Commission and chairman of its external relations group, and Mr. Henri Rochereau, the member of the Commission responsible for development problems, spoke in the debates. Finally, the EEC Commission sent a strong delegation of high-ranking experts from four different directorates general: external relations (D.G. I), economic and financial affairs (D.G. II), agriculture (D.G. VI), and overseas development (D.G. VIII).[2]

Theoretically, these three partially overlapping groups of delegates (member states, Council, Commission) were all working toward the same ends, and consequently they would be expected to coordinate their views and present a united front at the UNCTAD I meetings. In practice, this did not happen. A resolution on the results of UNCTAD I passed by the European Parliament in October 1964 took the Community to task on this lack of coordination:

The European Parliament. . . .

Regrets that the Europe of the Six was not able to benefit from this first important opportunity [UNCTAD I] to appear before the world as an economic unit and that the Commission of the EEC did not receive a mandate to represent the Community at the meetings of the conference as the Parliament had hoped;

Deplores the absence of effective coordination between the different positions of the member countries of the Community and stresses that the absence of a common attitude on the part of the member states could have extremely harmful consequences in the future for the harmonious development of world trade.[3]

This lack of coordination between the member states of the Community reflected a split into two camps on methods of aiding the developing countries. On one side, France, Belgium, Luxembourg, and, to a degree, Italy came out in favor of the so-called Brasseur Plan, which proposed a system of selective preferences. On the other, Germany and the Netherlands lined up behind the idea of generalized, nondiscriminatory preferences.[4]

Following UNCTAD I, the United Nations and OECD adopted special procedures to deal with the preferences issue. These affected the way in which the matter was handled in the Community. In the United Nations, in May 1965 the secretary-general convened a meeting of governmental experts from twenty-four countries (the Special Committee on Preferences) which included representatives from four of the EEC member states: Germany, Belgium, France, and Italy. In the Organization for Economic Cooperation and Development, a special group of four was set up to study possible offers to the developing countries. This group included two EEC member states: France and Germany.

The EEC Commission went to great pains to stress how much coordination existed between the four Community members of the Special Committee on Preferences. In response to a question from European Parliament member Pedini in April 1965, the Commission stated:

As it did at the world trade conference in 1964, the Commission permanently conducts exchanges of views with the governments of the member states. Normally coordination is achieved first in the Community institutions and then—with a view to harmonizing the viewpoints of the western industrial states—in OECD.[5]

Despite all this, the member states revealed a striking lack of harmony at the spring 1965 Special Committee meeting. The German delegation recommended a multilateral solution. The Belgians objected that a general, automatic system of preferences would be unlikely to solve the problems of underdevelopment and advanced the idea of setting up a system of temporary and degressive preferences in favor of certain products from the developing countries. France also came out strongly against the idea of general preferences without any quid pro quo. The French were very anxious to obtain worldwide commodity agreements for certain tropical products of particular interest to their former colonies. Consequently, they wanted to make acceptance of generalized preferences dependent on the negotiation of commodity agreements. Moreover, the French asserted that there should be no attempt to draw up a list of countries to which preferences would be granted, nor should the preferences be automatic. Italy, the other EEC member state on the Special Committee on Preferences, also wanted negotiation of the particulars.[6] In view of these sharp differences, it is difficult to see how the EEC Commission managed to claim that it had been able to inject an element of coordination and "Community approach" into the discussions.

Interviews conducted among national officials and EEC Commission administrators strengthened the impression obtained from the documentary evidence. The Community as a whole, it was claimed by some national officials, had no coordinated policy at all. In one interview, a high official went so far as to compare the Community to a drunkard, veering about with no discernible destination in view. In another interview the Community was compared to a boxer, jabbing here and stabbing there with no coherent action plan. Apparently, the Commission officials responsible for coordination had little contact with each other and were far too concerned with pushing the interests of their own directorate general to be able to do an effective coordinating job. In sharp contrast, those national officials interviewed regarded the EEC Commission's role as a necessary nuisance. Commission representatives, it was claimed, had to be dealt with for the sake of appearances more than anything else. The important matters, it was stressed, were initiated and settled, first on a bilateral diplomatic level and then, if they could not be settled bilaterally, were dealt with between governmental representatives.[7]

Similar intergovernmental disputes between EEC member countries occurred in OECD. Throughout 1965 the French and Belgians insisted on the need for selective preferences and were opposed by the Dutch and Germans, who favored the general preferences option. Italy, after several months as a rather lukewarm supporter of the French-Belgian line, finally veered round and joined the Dutch and Germans at the end of the year.[8] This Italian change of position swung the balance between the members and was largely responsible for the adoption in late 1966 of a Community position in favor of generalized preferences.[9] However, no sooner had this split been hastily patched over, than another issue divided the Community ranks once again: reverse preferences (the preferences certain developing countries grant industrial countries in return for advantages they obtain from the latter).

The issue of reverse preferences was of vital interest to the Community in view of its special treaty and traditional relationships with its eighteen African associates. As far as France was concerned, the Community had an obligation to its African associates; it claimed that reverse preferences could not be questioned. The Netherlands, on the other hand, favored the disappearance of all preferential systems like the one formed by the EEC-Yaoundé association. The Dutch position was, in fact, very close to that adopted by the United States in the Report of the OECD Group of Four published a short time before. The French position was understandable, since France was deriving the bulk of the benefits from reverse preferences. It was felt that Dutch opposition was based on a long-standing resentment that the French had made the other EEC member countries pay for the benefits extended to the former French dependencies under the Yaoundé association. In addition, the Dutch were embarrassed at the prospect of being tagged with French policies rather than Community policies, particularly in light of Indonesia's lively interest in generalized preferences. The result of this split between the Community governments was the failure to present a common position on tariff preferences in OECD before the opening of UNCTAD II in New Delhi in February 1968.[10]

In New Delhi, the Community faced very similar procedural problems to those it had faced in Geneva in 1964 at UNCTAD I. The six member governments of the Community were scheduled to be represented individually. The European Community, which the United Nations recognized as an "intergovernmental organization," could attend only as an observer, without voting rights. A common Community front was thus dependent on agreement among the member governments. Community circles were very concerned about this. The European Parliament, at its January 1968 plenary session, adopted the following resolution:

The European Parliament . . .

1. considers it essential for the Europe of the Six to present a united front at the second session of the United Nations Trade and Development Conference;

2. asks that the European Commission be called upon to act as spokesman for the member States at the Conference as regards all those areas that already come within the exclusive purview of the Community (tariff policy, agricultural policy, association treaties or trade agreements);

3. urges that the member States work out a common position concerning other sectors of Community interest and that this position should be expressed by a single spokesman.[11]

Despite this urging, the member states did not see fit to designate the EEC Commission as the Community's spokesman at New Delhi. In fact, the member states displayed what could be described as a split personality at the UN conference: in part they acted as a separate and distinctive entity, and yet they acted and spoke at the conference as individual nation states. For example, the heads of the delegations of the EEC member states each spoke in the general debate and gave his own country's views on development problems. However, Mr. Michel Debré, the French minister of economic and financial affairs, in his capacity as president of the Council of the EEC, began his statement with some comments in behalf of the European Community and then went on to speak in behalf of the French government.

The major Community problem at New Delhi was an awareness of the harmful psychological effect of failing to appear as a single unit at an international conference. This was made very clear in the European Parliament's follow-up report on UNCTAD II:

It is gratifying that the six national delegations of the countries of the EEC displayed an adequate identity of views during the debates. During the Conference, 28 coordination meetings were held between the national representatives and the delegates of the Commission of the European Communities. . . . Nevertheless, Europe of the Six was unfortunately not in a position, once again, to appear before the world as an entity. The six delegations spoke individually in the debates . . . it was the President of the Council who spoke officially on behalf of the Community in the general debate. The representative of the Commission of the Communities was not given a mandate to speak on behalf of the Community.[12]

One of the difficulties encountered by the Community states at

UNCTAD II was that they found themselves caught between two sets of cross pressures. One set was created by the difficulty of reconciling the Community's commitments to its eighteen African associates under the Yaoundé Convention with the strong political and psychological need to avoid the appearance of discrimination against the other developing countries. But the Dutch and Germans were much less enthusiastic about maintaining special regional preferences of the Yaoundé kind than the French, whose former colonial territories were involved. There is reason to believe that this particular split, which went back to the negotiation of Part IV of the Rome Treaty in the mid-fifties, was compounded by pressure from the United States. Apparently, American business interests were finding it difficult to get a foothold in the African countries, and some industrial lobbies were working actively to dislodge the French.

American concern with the closely related issue of reverse preferences provided the second set of cross pressures exerted on the member states. The United States had made it clear in OECD that it was going to take a strong stand in New Delhi against the Community's arrangements for reverse preferences. Whereas the French were strongly in favor of the maintenance of the reverse preferences at all costs, the Dutch remained somewhat skeptical of the need for the extra protection. If Common Market products could compete with those from other trade groups, the opponents of reverse preferences argued, they should be able to do so in Africa too. The issue was complicated further by a certain ambivalence on the part of the associated African states. On the one hand, they recognized that the reverse preferences could be used to obtain more concessions from the EEC, an important factor in 1968-69 with the Yaoundé Convention up for renewal. But on the other hand, the reverse preferences system, they claimed, obliged them to buy products they did not really want.[13] The African view was complicated further by the fact that many African leaders felt the need to submit a balanced set of demands for the Yaoundé association in order to retain Dutch and German support. The African countries felt that if they backed down on reverse preferences, the Dutch and Germans would be less bound to renew the association agreement.

The Community's need to reconcile the interests and demands of the African associates with the role of benefactor to all developing countries and, at the same time, to counter mounting American hostility to the alleged proliferation of limited preferential trading arrangements occasioned intensive intergovernmental negotiation from early 1969 to mid-1971. In January 1969 representatives of the Commission and the Permanent Representatives met with the ambassadors of the African associates for a round table discussion of the difficulties.[14] In March 1969, at a meeting of the Permanent Representatives Committee, EEC's executive secretary, Emile Noël, asked to have the item "negotiations with the associated states'' included on the agenda of every general Council of Ministers meeting during the ensuing months, for "psychological reasons."[15] After the Council of Association meeting held in April 1969, which was devoted almost exclusively to the preferences issue, representatives of the associated states met with Community representatives at least once a month to try to iron out problems concerning the generalized preferences.[16] Usually the more intractable problems were dealt with at the ambassadorial level. Other issues would be discussed informally by staff members from the African delegations and the EEC Permanent Representatives.

Difficulties with the United States were discussed in GATT. The director-general of GATT, Olivier Long, played an important part in smoothing over the differences between the two sides. Between July 1969 and May 1970, Mr. Long convened a series of private meetings between representatives of the EEC states, the EEC Commission, the United States, the United Kingdom, and Japan. On some occasions, representatives of the Scandinavian countries were also present.[17] Although Mr. Long was primarily interested in examining the legal implication of the generalized preferences proposal, he did provide a framework for intensive United States-Community consultations and paved the way for the final proposals to be submitted by UNCTAD's Special Committee on Preferences to the Trade Board in October 1970.

Despite a certain relaxation of tensions between the United States and the Community, lack of clarity in the American position on reverse preferences, which the United States was using as a bargaining tool, effectively held up finalization of the Community's proposals. In an account of a meeting of the EEC Committee of Permanent Representatives held in November 1970, at which the delegates were attempting to draw up a list of beneficiary countries, it was commented that no productive results could be obtained for some time, since the American position on the subject would not be known for a number of months. The Permanent Representatives concluded that they would have to confine themselves to discussing broad political issues, since there was not much point in discussing commercial and technical questions.[18]

At the same time as these difficulties in the international organizations, the EEC member states were locked in dispute until June 1971 over some of the more technical aspects of the EEC Commission's proposed system. There was particular conflict over the so-called Community reserve in the tariff quotas for sensitive products. Since it was held that the Commission proposal would benefit some member countries more than others, the Council rejected the proposal and engaged in a battle of wills with the Commission as late as mid-June 1971, a battle from which the Council emerged triumphant.

Viewed through the intergovernmental politics lens, the generalized preferences decision looks as if it was the EEC Commision's function to propose and the member states' privilege to dispose. However large and well-qualified the delegations sent by the Commission to the various international meetings, in the final analysis they were without real power to commit the Community to any particular line of action. So the member states were in a position of strength when it came to a battle of wills with Community bodies. With this background, it is hardly surprising that, in the traditional push-me-pull-you interplay between Commission and Council, most frequently the Council emerged the victor. It is only when the intergovernmental politics lens is exchanged for the other two conceptual lenses that we start to see different, more subtle forces at work.

Image II: The Interest Groups Call for Community Protection

In many policy areas, grass-roots pressures exerted on European Community institutions pass through a two-step process: interests are first articulated within the framework of local, regional, and national branches of organizations covering all sectors of industry; then, these branches take up the issue with the appropriate Community organs. In the generalized preferences case, a somewhat different process occurred. In this instance, EEC-level organizations of individual industries attempted to lobby EEC Commission members and administrators and Council secretariat personnel.

Industrial interests began to mobilize against the Community concept of generalized, nonselective preferences for all developing countries shortly before UNCTAD II. In January 1968, the Union of Industries of the European Community (UNICE), the Community-level body grouping together the national employers' associations, issued a strongly worded memorandum in which it specified clearly its objections to the proposed system. Moving from one international treaty obligation to another, the UNICE memorandum then maintained that the free trade system established between the member countries of the EEC and their African associates under the Yaoundé Convention should in no way be prejudiced. UNICE was not convinced, the report stated, that "preferences alone, as the developing countries expected, would have positive and certain economic consequences on the increase of their exports." It was necessary above all "to promote economically reasonable and sufficiently diversified industrialization in the developing countries."[19]

After these rather pious statements, UNICE quickly got down to the crux of the matter:

Generalized tariff preferences should not be granted to the developing countries without conditions, otherwise the donor countries would expose themselves to serious disturbances of their economies. . . . Consequently, UNICE considers that the industrialized countries must be in a position to forearm themselves against the disturbances that preferential imports could ultimately cause on their own markets, at the expense either of national products, or of products from other industrialized countries.[20]

Community employers were clearly afraid that generalized preferences might make some of the developing countries' industries uncomfortably competitive. They asked that the Commission draw up a list of exceptions, product by product and country by country; that the preferences be applied in the form of tariff quotas shared out among the donor countries; and that any preferences granted be temporary and degressive.

UNICE was responsible for defining and articulating general industrial policy and for lobbying all the Community institutions in Brussels. However, as it became clear that the Community was moving toward the institution of a generalized preferences system, both the national employers' associations and the federations of employers from industries likely to be particularly affected began to bombard Commission and Council secretariat staff with letters and to seek frequent meetings with high-ranking officials. Chief among these vulnerable sectors were the rubber, leather, cord, carpet, textile, and sewing machine industries. In November 1968 the Liaison Bureau of the Rubber Industries of the European Community sent a strongly worded letter to Axel Herbst, director general for external relations at the European Commission, to express its concern at the possible introduction of tariff preferences in the rubber sector. The Liaison Bureau claimed that generalized preferences to the developing countries would threaten the very existence of important branches of an industry that supplies products essential for the maintenance and development of a modern economy. The Liaison Bureau then adopted a somewhat threatening tone:

Our stand is strengthened by the fact that in most of these countries the main plants are subsidiaries of American firms which are the most powerful in the world and often control the source of their raw materials. These subsidiaries use cheap labor and benefit from a remarkable system of protective duties and quotas.

To underscore their argument, the rubber industries provided Mr. Herbst with a list of twenty-seven developing countries where the main rubber producers were subsidiaries of American firms: Firestone, General Tire, Goodrich, Goodyear, and U.S. Rubber.[21] In the same month, two more strong letters of protest came into the Commission, this time to the Commission's president, Jean Rey: one from the European Federation of Leather Glove Manufacturers and a second from the Federation of String, Rope and Cord Manufacturers.[22]

In late 1968 a number of national federations swung into action. In February 1969 officials from the Federation of Belgian Industries had meetings with Belgian government officials to express their anxiety over the EEC Commission's proposals on generalized tariff preferences. In a communiqué to the press, the Federation complained:

The EEC seems to be in the grip of a sudden fervour and is proposing practical details which go much further than was recommended by the United Nations. . . . To grant franchise for sensitive products, as the Commission proposes, is to jeopardize the very existence of part of our industry, without anyone knowing, in the long run, who will really benefit from this maximum tariff preference. [23]

The EEC Commission reacted to the employers' protests with a mixture of skepticism and reassurances.

Despite the reassurances, industrial concern built up as the EEC prepared to submit its offers to OECD in the first months of 1969. These offers, UNICE noted in a widely distributed February 1969 memorandum, were arousing considerable anxiety in many industrial circles in the Community. Since it was fairly clear by that time that the Community was prepared to institute a rather generous system of preferences, UNICE made a series of proposals that it considered essential for the protection of EEC industries. In any event, UNICE concluded,

the Commission's proposal . . . should be essentially conditional in character. The Community will have to be in a position to tailor its offer to the offers of the other industrialized countries. It is essential that a balanced burden be assumed by the donor countries so that European industry is not penalized.[24]

In the EEC Commission's detailed list of proposals, submitted first to the Council of Ministers for approval and then to OECD, an attempt was in fact made to allay industrial fears and to achieve a compromise between the numerous demands. The Commission adopted the approach that it was necessary to make generous offers in order to prove the Community's good faith and support for the developing countries. But at the same time, it did recognize that it had to take into account the sensitive position of some industrial sectors in the Community. The Commission was also concerned that the countries associated with the EEC should not bear the cost of concessions made to other developing countries. The Commission was not prepared, however, to respond to the pressures of the industrial groups to the extent of becoming involved in the negotiation of product-by-product exceptions from the system. In line with these guiding principles, the

Commission proposed an automatic preferences mechanism but, to quiet industrial anxieties, supplemented this with some exceptions and safeguards.

When the Council of Ministers, at its March 4, 1969 meeting, noted its agreement to the Community's communication to OECD, it also attempted to allay the fears of the Community's industrial sectors by stressing that the concessions should spread the load fairly.[25] One crucial area, however, was omitted from the proposals, since it was considered an internal Community problem—the list of sensitive products. Considerable controversy centered on such products as silk and woolen textiles, leather and skins, tires, cork items, carpets, sewing machines, and glass.

As the generalized preferences proposals went into their final stages, the textile sector became the source of greatest pressure on the Community institutions. Workers' organizations were also active. In June 1970 the Coordinating Committee of the EEC Textile Industries (COMITEXTIL) and the European Association of Clothing Industries submitted a joint declaration to the president of the Council of Ministers of the European Communities. The industries expressed their anxiety and called for a change in Community policy. They were particularly concerned that the EEC had made no provisions to exclude textiles from the system of generalized preferences, whereas the United States and the United Kingdom both proposed to do so. Moreover, since the United States was planning to adopt unilateral quota measures for textile imports, the Community would be exposed to increased exports from the Far East and the developing countries. The EEC textile and clothing industries called on the EEC to make its proposals consistent with those of the United States and the United Kingdom and to open negotiations in GATT on all textile products not covered by the Long-Term Agreement on Cotton Textiles.[26]

A few months later, at a round table in Amsterdam for COMITEXTIL representatives and labor union leaders, it was decided to send a telegram to EEC Commission President Malfatti to confirm the organizations' opposition to the Community's policy on generalized preferences. They asked for a meeting with the Commission president and also announced their intention of appealing to public opinion. The telegram was strongly worded:

The organizations of workers and employers in the textile industry in the European Community. . .

Note that, in spite of the various warnings by the trade, the policy carried out by the EEC authorities . . . is causing the greatest concern among workers and employers in the Community textile industry.

Cannot accept, in particular, that the EEC should alone make duty-free offers for textile products, when the major industrialized countries make exceptions of these same products, or, like the U.S.A., prepare new restrictive measures on imports.

Feel that they are obliged, at the request of their members, to draw the attention of the authorities and public opinion to the social and economic consequences of such decisions, as well as the responsibilities incurred, and have decided to undertake on this subject, a combination of actions on the Community scale as well as on the national level. [27]

In a separate communication, COMITEXTIL added:

Today it is a matter of *knowing* whether, while the U.S.A. has pronounced itself resolutely in favor of maintaining an important textile and clothing industry on its own territory, the Community intends to make a deliberate sacrifice of this industrial sector with the inevitable consequences:
—on the social level, uncertainty and redundancy for 3,200,000 workers
—on the economic level, irreparable losses
—on the trade and balance of payments level, an acute deficit
—on the political level, subordination in relation to outside for essential goods.[28]

The Community showed no signs of responding to this pressure during the last months of 1970 and the early part of 1971. In reply to a written question on the subject raised by European Parliament member Spénale in November 1970, the EEC Commission asserted that adequate provision had been made to limit the volume of imports admitted under the preferential system. It also pointed out that a permanent consultative body would be set up in OECD to follow trade developments closely after the institution of the preferences so that any necessary adjustments could be made. Finally, the Commission reassured Spénale that it had been keeping a close watch for some years on the international textile trade and the structural changes that had occurred in the sector and that it believed that the increase in the trade was beneficial to all parties.[29]

Reassurances of this kind did little to pacify the textile industry. In April 1971 the Round Table of Workers and Employers in the EEC Textile Industry again submitted a memorandum to all the Community institutions calling for the textile sector to be exempted from the generalized preferences system. The Round Table considered that the precautions and safeguard measures proposed by the Community were inadequate, and made a series of requests for more protective measures.[30]

Commission officials met again with employers' and workers' representatives at the end of April 1971 to consult on generalized preferences. Apparently, the industry's protests fell on deaf ears. In an indignant letter to President Malfatti "profound disappointment" was expressed. "The consultation," the letter declared, "was a pure *pro forma* exercise; it consisted in presenting the industry with a *fait accompli*."[31]

Not only the industrial sectors of the Community felt that they were being railroaded by the Commission and the Council. The European Parliament also indicated that it felt left out in the cold. In the June 1971 report drawn up for the Foreign Economic Relations Committee of the Parliament by the Dutch parliamentarian Theodorus Westerterp, the Committee complained:

Owing to the short time available, the Committee on Foreign Economic Relations is not in a position to go into detail into the background to the draft resolution which it is now submitting to a vote in the Parliament. . . . The Committee on Foreign Economic Relations regrets that it did not have the possibility of subjecting the draft regulation and the draft decision appearing in document 65/71 [the EEC Commission's proposals to the Council of Ministers] to a detailed analysis and of presenting amendments to these texts.[32]

In the June 9, 1971 debate in the European Parliament on the introduction of the generalized preferences, the members approved the proposals but voiced strong criticism. Many of the French members left before the vote in protest at the failure to exempt textiles. There was general disapproval of the differences in the offers made by the various industrialized countries. The fact that the preferences would not be introduced at the same time by all the donor countries was also criticized. The parliamentarians then went on to attack the Community's criteria for selecting beneficiary countries and its quota plans. Granting preferences to all the members of the Group of 77 meant that some developing countries would be refused preferences because they did not belong to the Group, whereas others that belonged to the group would enjoy preferences despite their fairly advanced economic development. As far as the quota plans were concerned, Mr. Westerterp, the rapporteur, insisted that under the proposed system an individual member state that accounted for the bulk of the Community's imports in a given product would be limited to much lower levels.[33]

The European Parliament voiced its objections less than two weeks before the Council of Ministers approved the various measures to implement the system of generalized preferences as of July 1, 1971. Although the system did contain certain safeguards and protective mechanisms, on a broad range of issues the EEC Commission and the Council of Ministers appear to have adopted somewhat strong-arm tactics and gone ahead with their concept of the way the generalized prefererences system should be set up and implemented. Some of the reasons for this will emerge from the next examination of the case.

Image III: An Inner Circle of "Preferentialists"

Although at first sight the generalized preferences case seemed an excellent example of intergovernmental decision-making, after interviewing officials from the EEC Commission, the Economic and Social Committee of the

European Communities, and the permanent representations in Brussels of both the EEC and associated African countries, it became clear that there was an extremely strong elite network functioning in the area. The network appeared to be centered on one section of the EEC Commission's directorate general for external affairs. (D.G. I.)

Very soon after the generalized preferences idea was launched in 1963, D.G. I became the focus of EEC Commission activity in the area. However, the nature of the subject necessitated a considerable amount of preparatory work in several other directorates general. A list of the administrative affiliations of the members of the EEC Commission delegation to UNCTAD I gives a good indication of this. The directorates general in the Commission are divided into directorates, which in their turn are divided into divisions. Officials thus rank in the following order: director general, director, division head, principal administrative officer. The delegation was headed by Mr. De Baerdemaeker, a director in D.G. I. The delegation's secretary also came from D.G. I. and bore the rank of principal administrative officer. The delegation had five counselors: Mr. Bosmans, a division head in D.G. I; Mr. Boyer de la Giroday, also a division head but in the directorate general for economic and financial affairs (D.G. II); Mr. Bertini, a division head in the agricultural directorate general (D.G. VI); Mr. Süssmilch, also from D.G. VI and a principal administrative officer; and Mr. Boissevain, a principal administrative officer from the directorate general for overseas development (D.F. VIII).[34]

All four directorates general just mentioned, together with industry experts from the internal market directorate general (D.G. III), dealt with the generalized preferences issue on a permanent basis from 1963 to 1971. However, it soon became clear that most of the pressure in favor of instituting the preferences was coming from officials in D.G. I responsible for general policy toward the developing countries, bilateral relations, and relations with the economic organizations of the United Nations. This group was headed by a dynamic Italian official, Matteo di Martino. He was aided by a small group of administrative officers who quickly gained a reputation, not only inside the EEC Commission but also at meetings of the various international bodies handling the generalized preferences, for being a closely-knit, highly effective group and past masters at both soft-sell and hard-sell public relations techniques.

This small group in D.G. I set itself apart to such a point that one high-ranking EEC Commission official dealing with some industrial aspects of the negotiations dubbed them quite spontaneously the "preferentialists." At another point in the interview he referred to them as the "inner circle." The "inner circle," he suggested, played their game with exceptional skill. Another official commented that the group presented the European Community to the world as a kind of "blue-eyed boy", although the project involved few real risks. They were also quite well aware that it would take a long time to surmount all the various difficulties that would inevitably arise inside the Community and in the international organizations. Among the member states of the Community, the D.G. I officials skillfully and persistently pushed their project, but, at the same time, they gave the impression that the project was not a first-priority issue. On the other hand, in the international organizations and in their relations with the developing countries, the emphasis was placed heavily on the Community's desire to participate in burden-sharing.[35]

This inner-circle element was apparently so strong that even within D.G. I itself there was a split between the "preferentialists" and the "others." The first group was headed by di Martino; the second, by another director, Axel Herbst. Apparently Mr. Herbst and his directorate were firmly convinced that nothing would come of the "preferentialists'" proposals and adopted a rather skeptical attitude about the whole question. As it became clear that the industrialized countries had to produce some tangible proposals at UNCTAD II to avoid exacerbating tensions with the developing countries, the "preferentialists" stepped up their pressure. Even on the practical level, the di Martino people had a reputation for doggedness, tirelessness, and sheer persistence on detail. As one official interviewed pointed out only half-jokingly, "They were terrific at hassling people, going around and knocking on their doors at all hours of the day and night."[36]

When the "preferentialists" were interviewed, a rather different impression was obtained, although the general tone was not inconsistent with the impressions of the "outsiders." Despite the fact that the Commission was only an observer at the international meetings, it was suggested that the real power was in fact in Commission hands. The Commission could in fact take advantage of its special status and "place the member states squarely before their responsibilities" by overcommitting them. This it could do because the Commission did not have a mandate and could not vote, so it had nothing to lose. In other words, it was suggested that Commission tactics were to present the member states with a *fait accompli* in the eyes of the rest of the world. It would then be far too embarrassing to go back on the Commission's word and display the Community's internal disunities in public.[37]

Despite the facade of harmony within the Commission directorates general, there were clearly fierce internal jealousies. One official described the rivalries as a struggle between the "foreign policy people" and the more "technical policy people."[38] Another EEC Commission official described the situation in slightly different terms: "The Commission has two hats," he said, "the trade hat and the charitable hat. When it is a matter of weight and influence on the world scene, D.G. I [external affairs] always wins out."[39] The rivalries between foreign policy staff and officials in other sectors also existed between Commission officials and national civil servants. As one EEC Commission official pointed out, the national civil servants felt that the whole area of aid was really their preserve and did not rightfully belong in Commission hands. Thus, there was a "constant wrestling match."[40]

These cross pressures between Commission officials and other interested groups also involved the lobbyists. From the outset almost all employers and a large number of labor unions in the industrial sector were bitterly opposed to the whole concept of generalized preferences. Even if they agreed in principle to preferential aid to the developing countries, they insisted that there must be exceptions for certain products and for certain countries. The lobbyists, however, were battling with the "preferentialists" from the EEC Commission on losing ground. The interplay was described by one Commission official as a game of ping-pong. The "preferentialists" would tell the UNICE people in Brussels that generalized preferences were an issue that had to be pushed by the national federations, and then they would tell the people from the national federations that the preferences were being pushed by the Commission on a Community level and that the whole matter had to be dealt with by the Brussels based people.[41]

These divide-and-rule tactics were apparently also adopted in D.G. I's relationships with the other directorates general, particularly with D.G. VIII (overseas development). However, there were indications that the "preferentialists" wished to keep the officials dealing with agricultural and industrial questions out of their bailiwick too. A series of memos circulated in D.G. VIII referred to the danger of allowing D.G. I officials to take over activities within D.G. VIII's province. They pointed up the necessity of careful consultations within the directorate general itself before embarking on any wide-ranging discussions with D.G. I. As D.G. VIII felt itself being gradually upstaged by D.G. I, it became increasingly jealous of its privileges and increasingly petulant. As one official put it: "What do you want? We [the officials in the EEC representing the interests of the African associates] are just the poor countries."[42] In response to a complaint from the director general for industrial affairs (D.G. III) that his own officials had not been invited to a meeting with representatives of the African associates organized by D.G. VIII, it was asserted that the Commission member responsible for development questions "had wanted to be able to meet personally and on a totally unofficial basis with the representatives of the associated states."[43]

However hard D.G. VIII tried to muscle in on the generalized preferences discussions, there was no doubt in most Community circles that the lion's share of the credit for positive developments regularly went to the "preferentialists" from D.G. I. As the Community's plans went into their final stages, at a meeting of the Committee of Permanent Representatives, in June 1971, Mr. Boegner, the French Permanent Representative, "thanked the Commission and, in particular, Mr. di Martino for the considerable work that the trade questions group had been able to achieve." Other delegations at the meeting also "stressed the importance and the precision of the work carried out by the Commission in so delicate an area."[44] What the Permanent Representatives did not praise was the superb piece of public relations work achieved by the "preferentialists," who had given the whole generalized preferences question so much publicity that the Community, after going beyond a certain point, was in no position to turn back without losing considerable face in the eyes of the developing countries and the rest of the world.

The three images of the generalized preferences case bring out very clearly how very subjective the analyst's view of decisional processes can be. If the events of 1963-1971 are observed through the intergovernmental relationships lens, one is left with the impression that the member states of the Community and the Council of Ministers were all important and that the other Community agencies—Commission, Economic and Social Committee, Parliament—counted for pitifully little. If we turn to the grass-roots or representative pressures lens, we tend to see a process of constant, dogged, sometimes even rather noisy efforts, efforts that admittedly were sometimes slow to meet with success, but which nonetheless left some mark on the final outcome. Finally, after observing the elite network in action and listening to their own and their colleagues' accounts of "how things really were," one is left almost 180 degrees away from the first impressions. The member states were indeed the voting members in the international bodies. The Council of Ministers was indeed required to give its final approval of the generalized preferences proposals. Yet, in the final analysis, the Council was by no means as powerful as the real policy initiators—a group of perhaps no more than half a dozen men who were well-known in many other parts of the EEC Commission and wherever the international organizations met as the European Community's representatives.

4

The Maghreb Association Agreements

Several features of the negotiations on the Maghreb association distinguish it from the generalized preferences case. First, the Maghreb countries had maintained strong traditional and commercial ties with France. In view of these special ties, the French government could be expected to maintain more than a passing interest in the progress of the association agreement negotiations. In addition, the other member countries of the Community had made concessions to France regarding its former dependencies in the negotiations of the Rome Treaty and were reluctant to agree to any further requests for a privileged status for former French dependencies. The Maghreb countries, as producers of Mediterranean commodities, were in direct competition with the southern regions of the Community, above all with southern Italy and Sicily. Preferential trading arrangements with Morocco and Tunisia could very easily put Italian producers at a disadvantage. Thus, a vigorous defense of Italian agricultural interests was to be expected in any EEC-Maghreb negotiations. Finally, the Maghreb countries, as integral parts of the Arab world, were very likely to bring strong opposition from pro-Israeli elements in the Community.

Image I: French Ties Versus Italian Fears

The association negotiations between the European Economic Community and Morocco and Tunisia lasted for more than five years. However, the procedures may be divided into a number of separate phases. When negotiations lagged, it was usually because at least one member state presented allegedly insurmountable obstacles to their successful conclusion; when negotiations moved forward, progress came from reduced tensions between the member states or from reduced difficulties in the relations between individual Community countries and the Maghreb states.

The first positive move toward negotiation was acceptance by the EEC Council of Ministers of the Moroccan and Tunisian letters requesting talks with the Community. This was followed by the Council's agreement to conduct exploratory meetings with representatives of the two applicant governments in 1964. This was undoubtedly a direct result of the end of the Algerian war, which made it possible for France to participate in negotiations. France's partners had also been unwilling until that time to get involved in any kind of politically delicate situation with the Maghreb countries. Even after the end of the Algerian war, difficulties presented by Algeria continued to affect Community relations with all three Maghreb countries. After the completion of the exploratory talks, it was necessary, in accordance with Article 228 of the Rome Treaty, for the Community's Council of Ministers to work out a mandate for the EEC Commission to negotiate on behalf of the Community. But under the Rome Treaty, any decision on the opening of negotiations with nonmember countries has to be approved unanimously by the Council of Ministers. Progress in this area was slow, particularly because, for many months, the question of Algeria was used by at least two of the member states to filibuster.

Throughout the discussions, Italy and Germany maintained that relationships with all three Maghreb countries must be treated as an indivisible whole. There was no question of working out separate arrangements for Tunisia and Morocco on the one hand, and for Algeria on the other. The Federal Republic was hostile to Algeria because it had supported the Cairo government when the United Arab Republic recognized East Germany. Morocco and Tunisia, on the other hand, had adopted quite conciliatory attitudes toward the Federal Republic throughout the entire dispute. So long as there was a chance that Algeria might recognize the East German authorities, the Federal Republic refused to allow the Community states to enter into commitments that could lead to agreements with the Maghreb countries. Italy, because of its severe agricultural problem in the south, was not prepared to face competition from any of the Maghreb countries. Consequently, the Italians were prepared to go along with any party that blocked the negotiations.

A partial breakthrough in the mandate logjam finally occurred in April 1965. In a communiqué issued at the end of the April 8 meeting of the Council of Ministers, only a very brief, passing reference was made to Algeria: "The Council has instructed the Committee of Permanent Representatives to start considering the report which the EEC Commission drew up after the end of its exploratory conversations with Algeria." However, the ministers expressed much greater enthusiasm with regard to Morocco and Tunisia:

After hearing a progress report by H. E. Ambassador Boegner on the work of the Committee of Permanent Representatives, the Council has instructed the latter committee to work out a negotiation mandate in liaison with Commission representatives. The Council has requested the Committee of Permanent Representatives to do its utmost to provide it with this mandate when it next meets. If this should prove impossible because of the short time this allows, the Committee of Permanent Representatives will nevertheless submit an interim report so that the *Council can finalise the negotiation mandate when it meets in June 1965.*[1]

At a press conference held after the Council meeting, Mr. Couve de

Murville, then president of the Council of Ministers, acknowledged in response to a question that negotiations could begin separately with each of the three Maghreb states. Apparently the Council had been able to make this policy change in response to a number of reassurances from the Algerian side. Mr. Couve de Murville had met with the head of the Algerian mission to the European Communities and had been informed that the Algerian government did not plan to recognize East Germany even if it did break off diplomatic relations with Bonn. On the other side, the Bonn government let it be understood that it would stop blocking negotiations with the Maghreb countries if Algeria did not recognize the Pankow regime.[2]

The first round of negotiations between the Community and Morocco and Tunisia took place in July 1965. This turned out to be the most inopportune time possible, since the talks came immediately after the French had walked out of the Council of Ministers, which resulted in seven months of near paralysis in the Community. Increasing tension between the member states prior to the walkout and, above all, increasing lack of cooperation by France, the chief backer of the Maghreb applications, meant that the Council issued the EEC Commission an extremely limited negotiating mandate. But even after the solution of the Community crisis at the end of January 1966, negotiations with Morocco and Tunisia made virtually no headway, mainly because the Italians continued to insist that negotiations with the three Maghreb countries could not be conducted piecemeal.

Italy had been opposed to the conclusion of special agreements with the Maghreb countries from the very outset. Most of the Maghreb's exports, above all citrus fruit, competed directly with Italian products. Any special arrangement with the Maghreb countries which led to an expanded market in the Community for their fruit and vegetable production presented serious problems for Italy. In addition, these problems were aggravated by the availability of cheaper labor in North Africa. As early as May 1964, the Italian government had circulated a paper among the member states in which it expressed anxiety about its fruit and vegetable markets. As the negotiations got under way, Italian anxieties mounted, and the Italian delegation frequently adopted an obstructive posture in the Council of Ministers. Even in July 1967, when suggestions came from both the Permanent Representatives and the EEC Commission on new mechanisms that would give partial protection to Italian production, the Italian delegation maintained its objections. Italy claimed that it wished to avoid a situation in which one member state of the Community would have to support the burden of concessions made to third countries. A product-by-product and country-by-country discussion, it was asserted, would each time isolate the Italian delegation in the negotiations, and Italy would gradually see its preferences for Mediterranean products melt away. Italy insisted, therefore, that overall solutions should be found that were valid for all sensitive items and for all Mediterranean countries.[3]

Italian proposals along these lines met with no support at all from the other member countries.[a] Nor was the Italian mood improved by some land compensation and fishing disputes with Tunisia, which had erupted at intervals since 1964 and caused strained relations between the two countries. However, after a series of bilateral negotiations, a meeting in Rome between the two foreign ministers, and the signature of three bilateral treaties in the fall of 1967, it was given out that nothing further stood in the way of a new era in relationships between the two.[4]

No sooner had Italian objections been removed by the signature of the bilateral treaties with Tunisia, than negotiation of the Maghreb agreements was held up once again by the new Middle Eastern situation created by the Six-Day War. There had in fact been concern over the EEC's relationships with Israel even before the June 1967 hostilities. It had been clear from the time provisions for the Maghreb countries were written in to the Rome Treaty that such preferential treatment would not only have trade implications throughout the whole Mediterranean region but would also create a political imbalance in the area.

Israel, at the same time as the Maghreb countries, had been pushing for special privileges from the European Community. Israel's efforts to obtain expanded privileges were vigorously renewed in 1967 when its first trade agreement, signed with the EEC in 1964, expired. However, the Six-Day War provoked a sharp EEC reappraisal of Israeli trade and aid requests. As one EEC Commission official remarked: "We suddenly realized that the poor Israelis, who were about to be severely handicapped by our projected agreements with the Maghreb countries, were in fact super-technicians."[5] As a result, a battle royal began between France, which had been pushing the Maghreb cause throughout, and the Netherlands, which, true to its consistently pro-Israeli policies, threatened to block the Maghreb agreements so long as Israel did not receive similar advantages from the Community. In its efforts to aid Israel and hold up the Maghreb agreements, the Netherlands had a steadfast ally in the Federal Republic.

Since Morocco and Tunisia quickly adopted a nonaligned position vis-à-vis Israel after the Six-Day War, whereas Algeria was more militantly pro-Arab, the Dutch and German action effectively ruled out conducting negotiations concurrently with all three Maghreb countries. Thus, by a

---

[a]Ultimately Italy did obtain some guarantees for its citrus fruit in the form of a protective price "cushion" which could not be extended later to other citrus-producing countries outside the Mediterranean area. It also obtained the EEC Commission's agreement that technical experts would be sent to the North Sea ports to study the difficulties encountered on the German and Dutch markets by Italian exporters.

strange turnaround, the Community was able to accept the principle of separate agreements. More flexible terms of reference were adopted by the Council in October 1967, and negotiations were resumed the same month.

Right up until the signature of the association agreements, the Dutch and Germans insisted upon parallel arrangements for Morocco and Tunisia and for Israel. This is undoubtedly one of the chief reasons why Morocco and Tunisia, faced with general Community foot-dragging and seemingly insurmountable opposition from the Netherlands and Germany, offered at the end of 1967 to settle for very partial agreements. Nevertheless, in July 1968, when the EEC Council of Ministers discussed a new negotiating mandate for the Commission, Mr. Luns, the Dutch foreign minister, continued the old policy. He made a strong point of maintaining a balance in the Mediterranean area as a whole and of pursuing Israel's candidature for association with the Community.[6] At the Council of Ministers meeting on December 10, 1968, Mr. Luns again linked the Maghreb and Israeli negotiations:

The Dutch delegation has already drawn the attention of this Council to the interdependence of our relations with the Mediterranean countries. We have seen today that we are no longer very far from concluding an agreement with Morocco and Tunisia. . . . We have unfortunately also to note, as I have said at the Council meeting on 30 July, that progress has not been as rapid with regard to Israel. Contrary to the promise that was made to us at that meeting, the Council has still not taken up the Israel application again. This is why I would again draw your attention to the fact that the Dutch Government cannot accept that Israel's request for association be neglected in favour of requests submitted by other countries in a similar situation.[7]

Even at the March 3-4, 1969 Council meeting, when it was perfectly clear that the Maghreb agreements would be signed within a week or two, Mr. Luns did not let up the pressure. A Dutch reservation asked for a negotiating mandate with Israel before final agreement was given to the Maghreb treaties.

The two agreements eventually signed by the EEC with Morocco and Tunisia in March 1969 were very different from the original proposals made by the two countries in 1964. On the basis of the available evidence, it seems reasonable to deduce that the persistent emphasis in the Council of Ministers on national economic and emotional considerations was largely responsible for the marked watering down of the agreements. Both the Maghreb representatives and the EEC Commission negotiators seemed firmly convinced that so long as provisions offensive to one or another of the member countries were not removed, there would be no agreements at all.[8]

An interesting sidelight to the negotiation of the Maghreb treaties was the extensive bilateral negotiations that took place at crucial times. Perhaps one of the most striking examples was the round of visits to European capitals made by Tunisian President Habib Bourguiba in July 1966. Mr. Bourguiba publicly stressed the importance to his country of concluding a special agreement with the European Community. He also stressed the moderate, pro-Western policy that had been adopted by Tunisia. Afterwards, it was noted in the press that he had considerably strengthened the Tunisian negotiating position in the Benelux and German capitals.[9]

Further Tunisian efforts to improve relations with Community countries were made in September 1967. Mention has already been made of the meeting between the Italian and Tunisian foreign ministers which led to the settlement of the land compensation and fishing rights problems. On the Moroccan side, in mid-1968 moves were made to unfreeze relations with France. The French had been at odds with the Rabat government on the grounds that it had been behind the disappearance in Paris of Mahdi Ben Barka, an opponent of Moroccan King Hassan's regime. On August 1, a Moroccan government delegation left Rabat for Paris to discuss the resumption of French financial aid to Morocco, which had been suspended for three years. The meeting seems to have considerably improved French-Moroccan relations.[10]

In this analysis of the negotiation of the Rabat and Tunis agreements, all the elements of the intergovernmental politics conceptual scheme are clearly present. Almost all the major steps were taken by the governments of the six Community states or of the applicant countries. In one case—the visit of President Bourguiba to the Community capitals—a major political move was made by the head of state himself. Ostensibly, at least, very little heed was paid to the wishes expressed by the other Community institutions. The EEC Commission constantly requested and was regularly denied broader negotiating mandates. It was also regularly denied provisions in the agreements for noncommercial advantages. The European Parliament was asked to express its opinions on the proposed agreements so close to the time of signature that it was too late for the parliamentary committees to research the matter thoroughly. After such lengthy and tortuous negotiations, the association agreements that finally emerged between the EEC and the two Maghreb states were based on minimalist concepts that served merely to save Community face and respect the letter of the provisions of the Rome Treaty.

Image II: Competing Products and Emotional Reactions

If the negotiation and conclusion of the Maghreb association agreements is viewed through the second conceptual lens, two major issues stand out: the threat to the fruit and vegetable-growing industries in southern Italy and Sicily; and strong pro-Israeli sentiments in the Netherlands and Germany.

From the very start of discussions between the European Community and the Maghreb countries, there was considerable concern among Italian fruit and vegetable growers that preferential arrangements with the North African countries would do further damage to their already declining economy. Growers in southern Italy and Sicily had no problems making their complaints heard, since farmers' representative organizations are large and possess considerable status in Italy. It is widely recognized both in Rome and in Brussels that the principal Italian agricultural organizations—the Confederazione Nationale dei Coltivatori Diretti (CONACOLTIVATORI) and the Confederazione Generale dell' Agricoltura (CONFAGRICOLTURA), which together represent close to two million farmers—exercise a strong influence on political events and government policy in Italy.

The Italian agricultural organizations also make themselves heard loudly and often in European circles in a number of different areas: by lobbying the EEC Commission (in the case of the proposed EEC-Maghreb association their targets were the external relations directorate general, D.G. I, and the agriculture directorate general, D.G. VI); by representations through their delegates to the Economic and Social Committee of the European Communities; and finally, by dealings with the "umbrella" organizations, or federations of national agricultural organizations.

In the case of the Italian fruit and vegetable growers' objections to the Maghreb association agreements, most of the lobbying was done on two levels. The organizations directed the bulk of their efforts toward the national ministries of agriculture and foreign affairs in Rome. The ministers then engaged in the three-year-long filibuster already described. They hoped to hold up the negotiation of agreements with Morocco and Tunisia by insisting that Algeria could not be treated separately from the other two Maghreb countries. This was of course done in the knowledge that two of the other member countries, Germany and the Netherlands, were totally unprepared, for other reasons, to conclude an association agreement with Algeria. Also, throughout the negotiations, representatives of Italian agricultural interests pressured D.G. I for safeguards to be written into the draft treaties prepared by the EEC Commission under its mandate from the Council of Ministers.

Other expressions of public feeling voiced in the national parliaments and the European Parliament focused almost exclusively on the need for a treaty with Israel to match the Maghreb treaties. However, it was difficult for the parliamentarians to criticize the particulars of the treaties, since the Council did not present the European Parliament with full texts of the agreements until March 18, 1969, less than two weeks before their signature. What is more, the parliamentary report on the agreements, drawn up by Mr. Bersani on behalf of the Committee on Relations with the African and Malagasy States, did not appear until May 28, 1969, two months *after* the treaties were signed. The result of this general lack of detailed information was that, on technical issues, there could be very little informed expression of public sentiment. It was only on the general principles that criticism emerged.

In the Dutch parliament in particular, a number of members protested the lack of parallel negotiations with the Maghreb countries and with Israel. In December 1968, Mr. Westerterp of the Catholic People's party put a written question to Mr. Luns, the foreign minister, about the need for more action on a Community agreement with Israel.[11] On February 27, 1969, Mr. Luns promised the second chamber of the Netherlands parliament that he would do everything in his power at the March 3 Council meeting to induce the Council to accept, when the agreements with Tunisia and Morocco were signed, the need to draw up a negotiating mandate for Israel.[12] Mr. Luns's efforts were not enough for some Dutch parliamentarians. Less than a week after the March 3 Council meeting, Mr. Dankert of the Labor party also put a question concerning the need to obtain Community action on the proposed agreement with Israel and linked this with the Maghreb agreements.[13]

In the European Parliament, pro-Israeli interests started mobilizing toward the end of 1968. At a meeting of the Foreign Economic Relations Committee in December, three Dutch members, MM. Vredeling, Berkhouwer and Westerterp, and Mr. Kriedmann, a German member, informed EEC Commissioner Martino that the Dutch and German parliaments would not ratify the EEC agreements with Morocco and Tunisia if the problem of Israel was not settled at the same time.[14] A month later, MM. Metzger, Vals, Wohlfart, Vredeling, and Dehousse, on behalf of the Socialist group in the European Parliament, submitted a draft resolution to the Parliament in which the Council was requested not to conclude any agreement with Morocco and Tunisia unless a similar agreement was concluded with Israel.[15] This resolution was submitted to both the Foreign Economic Relations Committee and the Political Committee of the European Parliament. It came before the plenary session for debate in February 1969. The European Parliament finally adopted a resolution that called for the observance of parallelism between the conclusion and entry into force of the Maghreb agreements on the one hand and signature of an agreement with Israel on the other. This resolution was adopted despite the fact that, in an effort at conciliation, the EEC Commission representative and some members (the Gaullists refused to stay for the vote) attempted to replace the principle of parallelism by that of a balance between the various agreements.[16]

The plenary session's resolution eased the pressure on two points: it did not call for parallelism during the negotiations, and it did not ask for the contents of the various agreements to be equivalent. However, both the Committee on Foreign Economic Relations, to which the question was mainly referred, and the Political Committee expressed their displeasure in the May 1969 parliamentary report on the Maghreb treaties. The Political Committee stated that it "deplored" the fact that the Council had not taken the Parliament's resolution into account.[17] The Committee on Foreign Economic Relations "expressed its regrets" on the subject.[18]

Thus, if we look at the negotiation on the Maghreb association agreements through the popular pressures lens, one issue only, the Italian fruit growers objections, is in sharp focus. A number of other issues, like the Dutch hostility to the agreements, are blurred, because there were few available means of bringing them into focus until the very last minute or after the fact. Although a fair amount of pressure was brought to bear by representative groups and parliamentarians, the EEC Commission and the Council of Ministers of the Communities paid little heed to their concerns. Even where interest group pressures appeared to bring results, these pressures were first filtered through the net of the national capitals and were then articulated in the EEC Council of Ministers—in other words, through intergovernmental politics.

Image III: Ambassadors and Eurocrats: The Gentlemen's Agreement

There is a fair amount of evidence to indicate that the negotiation of the Maghreb association agreements can be very neatly explained and understood in the framework of the elite networks conceptual scheme. Indeed, it was described by one high-level European Commission official, who had been working in the field of Community relations with the Mediterranean countries since 1957, as an "intimate little business."[19] Despite the Rome Treaty's declaration of intention concerning negotiation of special agreements with independent countries of the franc area, only France was seriously interested in strengthening the special links it already maintained with the the Maghreb countries. But France was not in any great hurry to conclude treaties. Its economic relations with Morocco and Tunisia were fairly good, and the problem of normalizing relations with Algeria was of considerably greater urgency than negotiation of association agreements with all three Maghreb countries. In any case, Algeria was considered the special domain of President de Gaulle, and he showed no signs of desiring any change in Algeria's trade relations with France's partners in the EEC.

It was not until 1967, after more than three years of very slow progress indeed toward agreement, that a small group of officials within the external relations directorate general of the EEC Commission (D.G. I) joined forces with the Tunisian and Moroccan ambassadors to the European Communities and made a concerted effort to speed up the negotiations. The small group of officials in question were able to take things very much into their own hands and work in conjunction with the Maghreb representatives for a number of reasons. The D.G. I group was made up of two types of officials. On the one hand, there were one or two highly experienced French administrators who had acquired their early training as French colonial officials in Africa. These officials had known for years most of the African diplomats, men who had been educated in French schools and in the French tradition. The relationship was not exactly an "old school tie" connection (after all, these were the former colonizers dealing with the decolonized), but there was a strong similarity of background, and the men involved apparently got along quite well with the Maghreb representatives. On the other hand, there were one or two young, extremely passionate "Mediterraneanists" in D.G. I who believed strongly that the European Community should maintain strong ties with all the countries of the Mediterranean area since it traditionally constituted an integral whole. The D.G. I group probably numbered no more than half a dozen, yet they were more than eager to make up for their lack of manpower in an effort to break the log-jammed negotiations.

On the Maghreb side, Ambassador El Goulli of Tunisia and Ambassador Guessous of Morocco had been in Brussels for a number of years, had worked with the D.G. I officials, and knew them well. In addition, they had a reputation as dynamic politicians and skillful diplomats. Above all, they worked together extremely well as a team. When the Mediterranean group in the EEC Commission and the Maghreb ambassadors, at a series of unofficial meetings, decided to move faster toward a set of agreements, teamwork became a keynote of the negotiations.

EEC Commission officials recognized the efforts of the two Maghreb ambassadors as one of the striking features of the later stages of the association negotiations. It will be recalled that between 1964 and 1967 there had been a number of cross pressures at work concerning the possibility of negotiating with each of the three Maghreb countries separately. Italy was particularly insistent during this period on the inopportunity of splitting the negotiations. On the other hand, there was considerable concern in most Community circles that due attention should be paid to the national sensibilities of the three Maghreb countries. Consequently, although all talks and negotiations with Morocco and Tunisia were conducted separately, very little time lapsed between the meetings, and the content of the discussions was very nearly identical.

Ambassadors El Goulli and Guessous paved the way for these negotiations with great care. They had repeated talks with the responsible officials in the member governments. They divided up the problems, persuaded, lobbied, and gathered support in previously neutral circles. This was particularly the case with the Belgian foreign ministry, which the Maghreb ambassadors managed to convert to a strong supporter of the association arrangements. They finally managed to convince key officials in all the member countries that it was better to go ahead with the negotiation of partial agreements and avoid a permanent stalemate. In the end, according to a Commission official, the new negotiating mandate of November 1967 was "cooked up by the Maghreb ambassadors and a small group of us in the Commission. It was pure politics. The actual agreements were quasi-formalities."[20]

As a result of the close ties built up between the two sides, the negotiators, once the talks got off the ground in late 1967, really took their responsibilities personally. On the Community side, during most of the negotiations, the delegation was headed by the Commision's director general for external relations, Axel Herbst. A late November 1968 report on the negotiations with Morocco underscores Mr. Herbst's approach:

Broadly speaking, an agreement seems to have been reached. I say "seems" because after a long morning's discussions between the Commission and observers from the member states, Mr. Herbst, who led the Commission delegation, "acted almost in a personal capacity" (to borrow his own words) in steering toward an agreement.[21]

It should be noted here that this was Mr. Herbst's last official negotiating activity before retiring from the Commission. It is obvious, in view of his impending departure, that he was eager to have the association agreements licked into shape as his final achievement. He was thus more than usually prepared, as the Commission spokesman pointed out, "to prefer taking the risk of seeking compromise formulas, which would allow the Commission to submit a final report to the Council, rather than take note of the differences and ask for time to think things over."[22]

Despite official reports of difficulties during the last few months of negotiation, EEC Commission officials seem to have been convinced that there were no real problems in finalizing the agreements. In fact, one person involved in the negotiations described the finishing touches to the agreements as a "procedural artifice." It appears most of the decisions were prepared in detail by the small group of negotiators from D.G. I and staff members from the Moroccan and Tunisian delegations. The bulk of the provisions were not even submitted to the entire EEC Commission. Strangely, it was only when the time came to sign the agreements that it was realized that there had been no formal agreement on the texts of the treaties: in other words, there had been no agreement according to the provisions laid down by the Rome Treaty.[23] The wording of one of the most crucial aspects of the agreements, the renegotiation clauses, was virtually meaningless from a legal standpoint.[24] Everyone knew this, it appears, and preferred to turn a blind eye rather become involved in further haggling. One official regretfully referred to this way of operating as belonging to "a golden age of the past" in Community affairs.[25]

After examining the Maghreb association agreements through each of the three conceptual lenses, it is clear that the intergovernmental politics lens provides a neat and tidy image. There is ample evidence to indicate that during most of the negotiations the pace was dictated by the prevailing intergovernmental climate in the Community. When relations were acutely strained in 1965 and 1966 the negotiations almost came to a standstill. In 1968 and 1969, when a much more cooperative spirit prevailed, the negotiations moved ahead. There is also evidence to indicate that a determined stand by one major government could also affect the negotiations. There were, however, limits to this. In the earlier part of the negotiations, when the issues were not clear cut, Italy, for example, held up activity for some considerable time. Later, in 1968 and 1969, even though both Germany and the Netherlands were not eager for agreements with the Maghreb without a similar agreement with Israel, and despite vigorous action in the Council by the Dutch foreign minister, the accords were concluded. Possibly, after six years of stop-go negotiations, the proposed agreements had become so watered down and innocuous that the Dutch-German opposition carried little weight. Moreover, all the negotiating parties were tired and needed to produce results.

It came as something of a surprise that there was so little solid evidence of the effective exercise of public opinion and interest group pressures in the negotiation of the Maghreb treaties. Although the Maghreb case in many respects resembled the generalized preferences decision, it differed in two important respects. Primarily, the conclusion of the Maghreb agreements was a strictly EEC-Maghreb affair and involved almost no external pressures. In contrast, in the generalized preferences case, the Community was faced with strong pressures in the international organizations to "do something for the developing countries." Opposition from public opinion and interest groups to the Maghreb treaties was also much less intense. It was much easier to pressure Italy into making concessions on the Maghreb treaties, particularly with France solidly behind the agreements, than it was to deal with opposition to generalized preferences from some of the most powerful industrial associations in the Community, which represented interests in all six member states. Even then, all the big guns of the industrial associations could only modify, not block, Community action.

Despite all these differences between the Maghreb case and the generalized preferences case, the elite networks images in the two cases were strikingly similar. In each instance, a small, highly motivated, extremely dynamic group of officials from the external relations directorate general of the EEC Commission pushed and pulled, manipulated and cajoled, literally "took over" when it looked as if negotiations would be interminably bogged down in intergovernmental wrangling. One of the interesting features that comes to light here is the effectiveness of such a small group of administrators against the weight of hostile or totally disinterested forces. Possibly their effectiveness lies in the very fact that the groups were small, could work constantly in close coordination, knew each other extremely well, and thus constituted extremely tightly knit units whose action was not dissipated or diffused in any way. Indeed, this explanation is in part borne out by the complaints currently voiced in all parts of the European Community bureaucracy that its size has cut down greatly on its effectiveness. This is not to say, of course, that the Commission has been taken over by mini-cabals in the various directorates general. But where a certain combination of temperaments and motivations exists, half a dozen men can produce significant results.

5 Free Movement of Labor

This third case study provides a rather striking contrast in scope to the cases studied in the two preceding chapters. Whereas generalized preferences and the Maghreb treaties were concerned primarily with external relations issues, the decision to abolish restrictions on the free movement of labor was almost a pure domestic question for the Community. In addition to the absence of external pressures, a second feature of the free movement of labor decision distinguishes it from the other four cases selected for study here. Free movement of labor measures predate the existence of the European Economic Community; detailed provisions were made in the treaty establishing the European Coal and Steel Community for free movement of workers in the two industries covered by that treaty. Also, this issue area was considered by all those associated with the founding and development of the European Community as one of the keystones of European integration. EEC Commission Vice-President Lionello Levi Sandri pointed out after the enactment of the final regulation in July 1968:

Free movement of persons represents something more important and more exacting than the free movement of a factor of production. It represents rather an incipient form—still embryonic and imperfect—of European citizenship . . . the complete liberalization of the movement of labour in the European Community constitutes a milestone and an achievement in the process of integration.[1]

Thus, a study of the free movement of labor decision of 1968 may give us important clues as to whether decisional processes are distinguished by any special characteristics when one of these "pillars of the creation of the EEC" is involved.

Image I: The Member Countries Look After Their Own Labor Markets

It should be borne in mind that the Rome Treaty provisions for the introduction of complete free movement of labor constituted a fundamental interference in the affairs of the member states. All the members naturally wished, in the event of labor difficulties, to give preference to their own workers. Although the minutes of the Rome Treaty negotiations are not available, it is known that the various delegations spent a long time over the social articles, which suggests that substantial difficulties had to be overcome.[2]

In addition to this basic encroachment on the sovereignty of the individual member states, certain fundamental differences of approach among the member states should be taken into account. Probably the most fundamental was the striking imbalance in labor availability between the six states. From the time the Rome Treaty went into effect in 1958 until the enactment of the final free movement regulations ten years later, Italy consistently registered a large labor surplus, whereas the other five member states experienced varying degrees of labor shortage depending on the region and the occupational sector concerned. The labor market did not remain static during the 1960s. Owing to extensive industrialization of northern Italy in the early sixties, and the natural tendency of workers to want to remain in their own country and avoid the problems of language and culture encountered when working abroad, there was a marked increase in movements from labor surplus regions in Italy to other parts of Italy itself.

Variations, at times considerable, also existed between the members' legislative provisions for workers' rights and benefits. For example, as far as provision of workers' housing was concerned, some Community countries (the Netherlands provides the most striking instance) suffered a severe housing shortage. Governmental authorities were averse to opening up workers' housing to non-nationals when there were insufficient accommodations for their own workers. Some member countries had elaborate restrictive legislation on labor union membership, wheres others had very little. France in particular had strict citizenship regulations governing membership and office-holding in labor unions. This put a considerable obstacle in the path of instituting complete equality between national workers and workers from other Community countries. Italy, the Community country most eager to see complete freedom of movement, had very little restrictive legislation. It was thus easy for Italy to push for the elimination of measures that favored national workers in other countries when it had no such discriminatory legislation of its own to abolish. Viewed from the other side, it was unlikely that France would wish to extend special benefits to non-nationals when Italy had no such benefits to extend in return.

Given this background, the picture that emerges from the intergovernmental politics lens is one of slow and very reluctant steps by the member states to implement the provisions of the Rome Treaty. There were frequent complaints from the EEC Commission and the European Parliament that the member states were showing insufficient interest in social questions. In a speech in 1964, EEC Commission Vice-President Levi complained bitterly:

It is natural sometimes to feel a certain dissatisfaction, particularly when we see all that has been done in other sectors and observe that the interest of the Member States is always drawn to more strictly economic matters in the sphere of general and international policy.

A few days ago the representative of a large member country laid before the Council his Government's views on what the Community should do in 1964. He hoped to see the development of closer relations with the non-member countries . . . greater importance given to economic and fiscal policies, a merger of the Executives and a strengthening of the powers of the European Parliament. He went more or less deeply into all aspects of the Community's activity. . . . But not one word on social questions.[3]

For long periods of time there were no meetings of the social affairs ministers at all. In December 1966, on the initiative of the Dutch minister for social affairs and public health, the ministers of social affairs of the member states of the Community met in a social council for the first time in two years.[4] Apparently, the situation had not improved very much a year later. The Social Affairs and Public Health Committee of the European Parliament, in its November 1967 report on the development of the social situation in the Community in 1966, was prompted to express the following regrets:

Owing to the insufficient activity of the Council of Ministers and the lack of cooperation between the member states, it regrets once again that no appreciable progress could be achieved during the past year. Consequently it earnestly requests the Council of Ministers of labor and social affairs to organize more frequent meetings with a view to reaching decisions which allow the gap to be closed between the social sector and the progress made in economic matters.[5]

In sharp contrast to these complaints of Council inactivity, frequent statements by various Community institutions point up the importance of social matters and emphasize the interdependence of social and economic development. Even some of the earliest Community publications refer to the free movement of labor as a vital contributing factor to economic and social progress. In the European Parliament's first report on the subject, drawn up in October 1960, much of the first chapter is devoted to a discussion of the interrelationship between the economic and social sectors. In order to move on from closed national markets to a common market and a real economic community, it was asserted, obstacles to the free movement of persons between the member states must be eliminated.[6] Some years later, in December 1966, a memorandum from the EEC Commission to the Council of Ministers on guidelines for work in the social sector also drew the connection:

The Treaty of Rome was manifestly designed with not only economic but also social considerations in mind. No other conception would in any case have been possible because of the close interdependence of economic and social problems and developments. . . . One has only to consider the developments in the Member States, where social considerations have played a decisive part in the determination of general lines of policy, to realize that the Community too must identify economic expansion with social progress and regard them as one and the same objective.[7]

The following year, in an opinion issued in October 1967, the Economic and Social Committee of the Community stated: "The Community considers that there indeed exists a close link between the future development of the Community's internal market and the free movement of labor."[8] Mr. Levi Sandri, in a statement made just after the final regulation passed the Council of Ministers in July 1968, also reaffirmed his faith in the necessity to promote social integration at the same time as economic integration:

Free movement of labor is not a simple corollary of the elimination of customs barriers; it is a feature of economic integration which [is] closely linked with the other aspects of economic integration: free circulation of goods, services and capital, constitutes the very basis of Community policy. . . . This principle is a logical and necessary consequence of economic integration. A different solution would have constituted an obvious and unjustified anomaly in the organic structure of the common market and an obstacle to its balanced functioning.[9]

Not only were the member states quite effective at going slow, they also appear to have battled successfully with the Community institutions on a number of occasions. The European Parliament was the principal victim of these struggles. In fact, under the Rome Treaty, the Council of Ministers was not required to consult the European Parliament, only the Economic and Social Committee. However, the Council did go beyond the Rome Treaty when the first regulation on the free movement of workers in the Community was being prepared, and requested the European Parliament, in August 1960, to give its opinion on the proposed regulation and directive.[10] The Parliament duly gave its opinion, but a report issued by its Social Affairs Committee a year later makes clear that it was convinced that its demands and recommendations were falling on deaf ears. The parliamentarians claimed that the member states had been particularly remiss in removing restrictions on workers' representation and the admission of foreign workers' families. They also complained that the member governments still set national priorities above the priority of the Community labor market. The Social Affairs Committee, the report stated, "charged some of its members with contacting various national ministries and requested its chairman to intervene personally and in conjunction with the Executive of the EEC with the governments which had raised special objections on these issues."[11]

The members of the parliamentary committee did indeed engage in the active lobbying recorded in the report. Nonetheless, the issue of priority for the Community labor market continued to cause problems with the representatives of the member governments in the Council. Unable to achieve results by exhortation and gentle reprimand, the committee then decided to send a letter to the president of the council of Ministers which set out its disagreement with the Council's proposals. It also asked its rapporteur to follow the preparation of the Council session with particular attention. Despite these watchdog measures on the part of the Parliament, the Council of Ministers adopted a version of the regulation mainly based on a minimalist compromise proposal submitted by the EEC Commission, which did not go nearly as far as the suggestions made by the European Parliament in its proposal.[12] The parliamentary Social Affairs Committee duly registered its complaint:

We note a distinct difference between the two texts: the text which was originally proposed by the EEC Commission and which was adopted by the European Parliamentary Assembly and by the Economic and Social Committee of the Community; and the text which was finally adopted by the Council of Ministers.[13]

Only very slowly did the member governments agree to the introduction of priority for the Community labor market and thus accept the loss of their national sovereignty. Under the 1961 regulation, workers had to have specific job offers before they could go and work in another country. In the second regulation of May 1964, some advances were made in denationalizing the individual labor markets of the member states and introducing the elements of an overall Community system, but the measure was only partial. Under the 1964 regulation, after considerable negotiation, the members agreed that a foreign worker need be employed for two years only (as opposed to four years under the old regulation) before he was permitted to engage in other wage-earning occupations in his host country. It was not until the final regulation passed in 1968 that the concept of the priority of the national labor market was dropped completely and non-national workers were given very nearly the same rights and privileges as national workers.

A detailed analysis of the July 29, 1968 meeting of the Council of Ministers, which passed the final measures to introduce complete mobility of labor between the member countries of the Community, underscores the strains and tensions that existed between the six states in this area even after almost a decade of legislation. As a prelude to this, however, it should be pointed out that in the spring of 1966 the Council of Ministers decided to introduce the free movement of industrial and agricultural goods by July 1, 1968, eighteen months earlier than had been provided for in the Rome Treaty. In May 1966, Italy called for the free movement of workers to be guaranteed for the same date.

Italy, it will be recalled, was the only member country of the Community with a big labor surplus. Since the inception of the EEC, it had assiduously pushed for liberalization of labor movement legislation in the Community. The other member countries had always been wary of Italian moves. However, by mid-1966, it was well known that Italian workers from Sicily and Calabria were moving in increasing numbers to northern Italy owing to growing industrialization in the region. In addition, other member countries, particularly Germany and France, were beginning to absorb more and more workers from outside the Community, chiefly from Portugal, Turkey, Yugoslavia, and Algeria. Consequently, less pressure from Italian workers combined with growing pressure from non-Community workers made the Italian move in May 1966 much more palatable to the other member states. Acceptance of accelerated implementation of the free movement of labor provisions of the Rome Treaty did not, in fact, make any real demands on the member states.

Despite the greater willingness of most member states to institute free movement of labor within the Community, the 1968 measures did not have an easy passage. The ministers devoted an entire morning to discussing the three most difficult problems under consideration: the representation and eligibility of foreign workers in labor union organizations; the provision of a safeguard clause in the event of serious disturbances on the labor market in a particular region or occupation; and the requirement that foreign workers have housing accommodations before they send for their families.

The problem of immigrant workers' elibigility to vote and stand for election in labor union organizations in the country where they worked gave rise to a heated and lengthy discussion in which the French delegation took a vigorous stand against the extension of union rights to immigrant workers. French law stipulates that leading positions in labor unions can be occupied by French citizens only and that board members of labor unions can occupy posts on an ex-officio basis in the public administration as, for example, in the management of social security funds.

The main thrust of the demands for nondiscrimination came from Italy, which had no national legislation in this area. Italy was thus asking for rights for Italian workers in other European Community countries when it had no such guarantee for its workers at home.

The safeguard clause presented an institutional problem. All the member states thought it necessary to mitigate the effects of complete free movement of labor in regions already affected by unemployment. The Italian government and the EEC Commission maintained that the decision should be taken by the EEC Commission. The German and French delegations, on the other hand, suggested that the decision should be taken by the Council of Ministers acting on a proposal from the EEC Commission. The housing problem was thorny, but it was the only one settled during the morning ministerial session. On a French proposal, it was agreed that workers with accommodations "considered normal" would be able to send for their families. Apart from this, no discrimination would be allowed between national workers and workers from other Community countries.

When the ministers returned to the Council in the late afternoon, they immediately postponed discussion of the contested questions once again until the end of the meeting in the hope that a "package" discussion would produce an overall compromise. However, it was only after lengthy discussion that compromise procedures were finally agreed upon. As for the safeguard clause, it was decided that the government concerned would submit its request to the EEC Commission, which would have two weeks to reach a decision on the matters. The other member states would then have two weeks in which to appeal to the Council of Ministers from the Commission decision. Finally, the Council of Ministers would have a further two weeks to give an answer to the appeal. Because of the strong national pressures, the compromise that evolved was extremely elaborate, with provision for small portions of authority to be exercised in turn by the national governments and by Community institutions.

The compromise on labor union rights, also evolved after a long battle, took French sensibilities very much into consideration. It was decided that Community workers could have the right to vote and to serve on workers' representative bodies on the same terms as nationals. Provision was made, however, to exclude access to certain labor union posts that might involve participation in the management of a public service or department. But final settlement of the matter was left in partial abeyance. It was agreed that the Council would insert a revision clause in the regulation providing for reexamination of the problem after two years.[14]

Up to this point in the analysis, attention has been given almost exclusively to the activities of the member states in asserting their individual interests in the Council of Ministers in opposition to the wishes expressed by the EEC Commission, the European Parliament, and the Economic and Social Committee of the Community. The strong bargaining position of the member governments and the relative weakness of the Community institutions was amply confirmed when officials from labor unions and representative groups in industry were interviewed.

Despite the fact that all the proposals for free labor movement legislation came from the EEC Commission, and the Council was also required under the Rome Treaty to consult the Economic and Social Committee, it was generally asserted by representatives of labor and industry that lobbying the Commission and expressing views in the Committee had little payoff. This was particularly true, it seems, after the 1965-66 crisis in the Community. It became increasingly obvious that the major problems were settled between governmental experts, frequently on a highly personal basis, in the Committee of Permanent Representatives or, in the last resort, in the Council of Ministers itself. The labor unions and employers' federations consequently turned their efforts increasingly to the national governments. As one labor union official points out, "We did not really want to turn in that direction, but we found ourselves obliged to do so."[15]

The intergovernmental politics lens thus provides an image of a process in which the member governments, from the outset, made nothing more than a show of listening to the EEC Commission and consulting representative Community bodies like the Economic and Social Committee and the European Parliament. With the passage of time, decisions became increasingly dominated by rival national concerns as, for example, Italian needs to find outlets at optimum conditions for their surplus labor.

It would be legitimate to suppose that in an area close to the lives of the ordinary Community citizen, and in legislation affecting the rights and privileges of individual workers, expressions of public and representative group opinion would have been more clearly heard. If the lenses are switched and the free movement of labor decision is viewed through the second lens, a somewhat clearer, though admittedly still hazy, picture is obtained of the place of grass-roots and interest group views in decisional processes.

Image II: Freedom of Movement Becomes an Individual Right

It will be recalled that although Article 49 of the Rome Treaty provided for the Council of Ministers of the European Community to consult the Economic and Social Committee before it enacted measures concerning free movement of workers, it did not require any consultation of the other body closest to Community grass roots—the European Parliament. However, even when the first regulation on the free movement of workers in the Community was being prepared, the Council went beyond the letter of the Rome Treaty and, on August 8, 1960, requested the European Parliament to give its opinion on the proposed regulation and directive.[16] When the Parliament issued its opinion in November 1960, it reminded the Council of Ministers that it wanted to continue to have a say in free movement of labor decisions: "It expects also to be consulted when future regulations and directives are formulated with a view to the second stage which will fully implement the aims set out in Article 48 of the treaty establishing the EEC."[17]

In a supplementary report issued by the Social Affairs Committee of the European Parliament a year later, the parliamentarians explained in some detail how they had kept a very close eye on the discussions in the various institutions:

The texts adopted during the plenary session of October 15 were then sent to the Council of Ministers. But the Social Affairs Committee considered that its role in this area did not stop there. Fully conscious of the political importance of the participation of the Assembly in the procedural mechanism set in motion for free movement, the Committee has followed closely throughout these past months the work of the Council of Ministers, from the discussions in the various working groups to the final adoption of the texts at the June 12, 1961 session.[18]

The report describes how the Social Affairs Committee decided to lobby the national ministries of labor and social affairs and the secretariat of the Council of Ministers concurrently. The parliamentarians made these contacts on a personal level in the national capitals, but engaged in a written exchange with the president of the Council of Ministers. They were particularly concerned that the Council was not moving ahead swiftly enough or paying adequate attention to certain specific areas, particularly Community labor market priorities.

Parliamentary lobbying was quite intense but, as indicated in the first analysis, brought far fewer returns than hoped. It should not be forgotten here that the parliamentarians were struggling again against a great weight of governmental reluctance among the member states to give up any part of their national priorities. Consequently, although the gradual elimination of national priorities in the subsequent regulations seemed slow and tortuous when viewed through the intergovernmental politics lens, it was viewed as a considerable triumph by the proponents of a Community-wide labor market in the European Parliament.

The second regulation of May 1964 made some striking advances in denationalizing the individual labor markets of the member states and in introducing the elements of an overall Community system. A worker from another Community country had only to work in the host country for two years before he could engage in any other wage-earning activities. It was also made much easier for the foreign worker to bring his family to join him in the host country. By the time the 1968 regulation was passed, the concept of the priority of the national labor market was dropped almost in its entirety, and non-national workers were given very nearly the same rights and privileges as national workers. In addition, under the 1968 regulation, a safeguard clause that permitted the reestablishment of national priority for workers could only be invoked if multilateral procedures were set in motion within the framework of Community institutions.

Members of the European Parliament, particularly socialists, were also quite active individually through parliamentary questions to European Community institutions. Dutch parliamentarian Nederhorst, for example, regularly questioned the EEC Commission on labor matters. With regard to the 1961 regulation, there was some concern about the lack of publicity. Mr. Nederhorst consequently took the EEC Commission to task and asked whether it was aware that workers occupied in a country other than their own were almost completely ignorant of the provisions of Regulation No. 15 and the rights that it conferred on migrant workers.[19] The question prompted an unusually vehement and defensive response from the Commission.

Stress on individual workers' rights moved more and more into the foreground as the 1960s progressed. In fact, there was what seems a rather broad change in EEC philosophy with regard to labor movements. The relevant Rome Treaty provisions suggest that the philosophy of the mid and late 1950s was one of equilibrium between supply and demand. As the European Community gradually evolved, it became clear that an attempt was being made to drop this restrictive interpretation of free labor movement. In March 1964, EEC Commissioner Levi Sandri spoke on the topic "Geographical and Occupational Mobility of Workers in the Framework of a Common European Employment Policy" at the fifth meeting on the problems of European integration held in Florence by the Italian Federation of Labor Unions. In his speech, Mr. Levi Sandri explained that the free movement of workers had progressively been elevated from merely a way of abolishing unemployment and promoting a balance between labor supply and demand, as had originally been intended when the Rome Treaty was drafted, to a fundamental right of the individual.[20]

This aspect of fundamental individual rights was given considerable emphasis in the July 1968 measures. The labor permit for Community nations that had existed under the previous legislation was replaced by an EEC identity card, valid for at least five years and automatically renewable.[21] The Social Affairs Committee of the European Parliament, in its October 1967 report on the proposed directive, highlighted this feature.

It should be noted that [the proposed directive] is moving in the direction of introducing an identity card for migrant workers, which represents, on a more general level, a symbol worthy of being underlined. The Social Affairs Committee gives its backing to this EEC proposal which can be a model that goes beyond the framework of the free movement of labor and which may constitute the first rough model of European nationality.[22]

The issue of individual workers' rights would not have received so much attention had it not been for the efforts of the Community labor unions. From the outset they made determined efforts to act as watchdogs. In addition to action by the national labor unions in their own capitals, the European federations in Brussels met with officials of the social affairs directorate general of the EEC Commission, the secretariat of the Council of Ministers, and the Social Affairs Committee of the European Parliament. Parliamentarian Rubinacci, in his 1961 report for the Social Affairs Committee, stated:

It was considered indispensable to hear the opinion of employers' and workers' representatives on two occasions. Your committee considers that this initiative is a particularly gratifying one, for it is convinced of the necessity of associating as often as possible those industrial sectors—above all those concerned with the problems of free movement of workers—with the work of formulating draft proposals dealing with this problem.[23]

The legislation on free movement of labor also made provision for involving representative groups in Community activity. Under the first regulation, enacted in 1961, two advisory committees were set up. One of these, the Consultative Committee on the Free Movement of Labor, was a tripartite committee composed of representatives, in equal numbers, of the national governments, labor, and employers. The Consultative Committee was maintained under both the 1964 and the 1968 regulations. Through their representatives on the Consultative Committee, workers were able to make some of their wishes and concerns known. The Consultative Committee worked primarily with the EEC Commission and was to a certain extent dependent on it. Greater initiative was taken by the labor unions and the employers' federations through their European-level confederations. In a 1964 speech, EEC Commissioner Levi Sandri drew attention to these organizations:

Some of the trade unions and employers' associations have already adapted themselves to the dimensions of the Six. European secretariats and liaison offices have been established to bring together the organizations in the Member States in a spirit of sincere co-operation with the Community institutions. This is the first step toward the establishment of true European organizations.[24]

A year later Mr. Levi Sandri made a public appeal for even greater coordination on the European level. The time had come, he said, to move forward from secretariats and liaison offices to proper organizations so that the structure of social institutions should not lag behind the economic integration of Europe.[25]

A pointer to the close contacts maintained with the Council of Ministers by the labor union federations and the employers' organizations may be seen in the crucial July 29-30, 1968 Council of Ministers meeting. It was at this time that the final measures on the free movement of workers were enacted. The proceedings began with a statement from the chairman on the talks he had held during the morning of July 29 with representatives from the labor union and employers' organizations. The chairman, the Italian ministers of labor, reported to his colleagues that the labor unions had been particularly emphatic in their demands for full recognition of all labor union rights for Community nationals working in other countries.[26]

This second look at the free movement of labor measures reveals that the forces at work in initiating, drafting, and modifying legislation were much broader than they would appear if action by the member states and in the Council of Ministers alone had been examined. It is particularly interesting to note that pressures were exerted most successfully in those areas that were not always the most obvious. Although the Rome Treaty provided for consulting the Economic and Social Committee of the Community, there is little real evidence that it did much to change minds significantly. The European Parliament was invited by the Council to give advisory opinions on draft legislation in the area, and the parliamentarians made a point of pressuring the ministers to continue this consultation. Yet, despite quite a lot of noise from the parliamentarians, there is not much to suggest that the European Parliament was any more successful than the Economic and Social Committee. Finally, in the one area where specific provision was made for representative groups to work with Community officials—in the Consultative Committee on the Free Movement of Labor—interviews indicate that the representative groups did not put much faith in the effectiveness of either the Committee or the EEC Commission. As one labor union official remarked rather cynically, "The EEC Commission was not aware of its own limitations and did not fully realize that it was not in a position to carry out its plans."[27] In contrast, much of the effective pressure was exerted by organizations that had not come into being in 1958—the European-level federations of labor unions and employers' organizations—on a body that was not really intended to be the chief instrument for putting integrationist policies into effect—the Council of Ministers.

Image III: The Socialists Combine

In the two previous chapters, the third conceptual lens revealed that an extremely influential role in decision-making was played by a small group of officials in the EEC Commission. Neither the documentary evidence nor personal interviews reveal any such pattern in the present case. However, a very different, much less well-defined pattern of group dynamics did emerge, focused on Lionello Levi Sandri, the member of the EEC Commission in charge of social affairs. The commissioner, later the vice-president of the Commission, pleaded the cause of European social integration with great dynamism and considerable zeal. In a speech early in 1964, typical of many he made, Commissioner Levi Sandri declared:

We know that the Common Market is not an end in itself. It is only the basis and the prior conditions for a deeper and closer integration of the European peoples. . . . the European ideal must not be the monopoly of limited circles of initiates and specialists but the common patrimony of our generation and of our peoples. . . . The European Community must be a genuine instrument of social justice and must be seen to be such by the working masses, who form the great majority of our population. These people will then be led more and more to identify their needs and hopes for work and justice with the progress of European integration.[28]

The commissioner's public pronouncements suggest a man thoroughly devoted to the idea of a united Europe. His strong socialist background also strengthened his focal position. Before he was appointed to the EEC Commission in 1961, Mr. Levi Sandri was an active member of the Italian

Social Democrat party. Not only had he served on its executive committee, but he had also been a member of the National Committee of the united PSI-PSDI (Italian Socialist party-Italian Social Democrat party). He had been head of the executive staff of the Italian minister of labor and participated in many international meetings and committees enquiring into such problems as social security and labor law. He was, therefore, a prominent European, as well as Italian, socialist.

Many of the other active exponents of free movement of labor in the European institutions, particularly in the European Parliament, were also socialists and active labor unionists. This is true for many of the most vocal members of the Social Affairs Committee of the European Parliament (chairmen, rapporteurs, and questioners). Mr. Alfred Bertrand, a rapporteur on free movement of labor in the time of the European Coal and Steel Community and rapporteur for the first EEC discussions on the subject, was provincial president of the Christian Workers movement of Limbourg. Mr. Leopoldo Rubinacci, the rapporteur on both Regulation No. 15 of 1961 and Regulation No. 38 of 1964, had been co-secretary of the Italian General Confederation of Labor, Italian undersecretary of state for labor, minister of labor, and chairman of the Italian parliamentary committee of enquiry into the situation of workers in Italy. In these various positions, he had come into close contact with Mr. Levi Sandri and learned to work well with him. Mr. Gerard Nederhorst, for a number of years chairman of the Social Affairs Committee and always an outspoken and vigorous protector of migrant workers' rights, was a member of the socialist group and special attaché to the Dutch Federation of Labor Unions. Mr. René Pêtre, rapporteur for the 1968 regulations, was general secretary of the Free Miners Organization of Belgium.[29] With this kind of leadership in the Social Affairs Committee, it is hardly surprising that the committee maintained good relationships with the EEC commissioner in charge of social affairs. It is also not surprising that parliamentary committee activity in the social field, although frequently not as effective as the parliamentarians would have liked, made more of an impression than in most other areas of Community concern.

Aside from this solidarity between the socialist and labor union members of the European Parliament and the EEC commissioner, there is little to indicate that Mr. Levi Sandri was able to rally a circle of followers around him in D.G. V as, for example, his colleague Sicco Mansholt was doing in the agriculture directorate general. A distinct impression was obtained from several interviews that D.G. V had a reputation for being one of the more lethargic and less inspired of the EEC Commission's subunits. It was even accused by some observers (especially in the unions) of being more a hindrance than a help in pushing through social legislation. Despite the fact that the Rome Treaty had given the EEC Commission broader social powers than in many other areas, it seemed to be able to do little in the face of the amassed power of the ministries of the member states.

Another explanation for the Commission's alleged inability to act effectively may lie in the ingrained hostility of the labor unions toward bureaucracy. Labor union officials, usually men with a long background of struggle on the national level for improved conditions for workers, were not unnaturally suspicious of bureaucrats from the EEC Commission voicing high-minded European ideals and, what is more, in public—a new mode of behavior altogether for bureaucrats. As far as many of the labor union men were concerned, the EEC Commission was pursuing impractical dreams, while the unions were doing the spadework in trying to get together some form of down-to-earth, coordinated labor policy. It was even suggested that the Commission departments were wasting their time on formulating plans that could never be put into effect.[30] It is not surprising that the unions were not as reluctant as they sometimes seemed to lobby the national ministries rather than the EEC Commission. Moreover, although the unions expressed some eagerness to see the promotion of social integration in the European Community, it was another story when they were faced with extending hard-won national rights and privileges to workers from other Community countries when these countries did not necessarily extend similar rights and privileges to their own workers. Consequently, one sees very little evidence of active politicking by the national labor unions with their own governments, except in the case of Italy.

It is possible to say, after conducting this examination of the free movement of labor decision, that there were some elements of an elite network in operation. However, the network was not tightly knit, and its composition was rather unusual—the Commissioner and labor experts in the European Parliament. Although the group was noisy, it was not very effective. It seems, therefore, that in areas where there are strong governmental and interest group pressures militating against swift action, an institutionally heterogeneous group, however dedicated to the cause, makes only a slight impact on decision-making processes.

The three-lens analysis of the free movement of labor decision produced some rather unexpected results. One of the most important findings to emerge was the strength of nationalism and the extent of intergovernmental rivalries over a program to which all the member states were committed through their signature of the Rome Treaty. It was also rather surprising to discover that the member states most of the time rode roughshod over the Community institutions on this question. Free movement of labor could not be labeled a "high" politics issue by any stretch of the imagination. Yet the institution that should have been most prominent in this domestic area of integrative measures, the EEC Commission, appears to have played a rather insignificant part.

Not only did the member states maintain the upper hand, but their debates seem to have been most acrimonious over such precise and detailed topics as housing and specific labor union rights. There is no indication that the member states were being hypocritical over the eventual institution of free labor movement. They were each struggling to safeguard as many of their own interests as possible with as little sacrifice as possible.

Another rather unusual feature was the small amount of noise made by the different Community institutions. The EEC Commission's departments, in sharp contrast to the two previous studies, do not seem to have had much impact on decisional processes. There is little evidence of activity between Council meetings (which were infrequent) and little to indicate that the Commission played a prominent conciliatory role between the member states. It seems as if the social affairs directorate general suffered from a slight feeling of inferiority and bent more easily to pressures from the national governments.

If EEC Commission officials were surprisingly quiet on the free movement of labor, the European Parliament was unusually vocal. There seems to be direct link here with the grass-roots nature of the subject matter. Free movement of labor raised such fundamental questions as whether the worker could bring his family to join him in another country and what kind of housing accommodations he could expect. It is not in the least surprising that socialist and labor union parliamentarians insisted on having their say on such questions, whereas members of the European Parliament were prepared to be very much quieter on foreign relations issues that affected their constituents and ideals much less directly.

The final surprise was the absence of a strong elite group working for the free movement of labor. Despite rousing speeches from Commissioner Levi Sandri and firm pronouncements from the Social Affairs Committee of the European Parliament, only a very loose alliance developed between the two. The fact that Italy was seen in Community circles as pushing for free movement because it had most to gain from such measures may have led some to believe that Mr. Levi Sandri was bent on feathering his own national political nest. On the other hand, without strong backing from his own officials, a commissioner has much greater difficulty in building up an alliance with representatives of other institutions.

6 Agricultural Structures

When the Council of Ministers approved the "New Guidelines of the Common Agricultural Policy" at the end of March 1971, they agreed to a package of proposals that had caused more controversy in the European Community than any other program in its history. No Community government wanted to pay out too much for the benefit of the other five. Also, there was conflict between the French, who as the Community's chief agricultural producers stood most to gain from the structural reforms, and the Germans, who did not wish to foot the French bill and were more interested in prices than structural reforms.

Within each of the six member governments there were conflicts of interest and priorities. The foreign ministers claimed that such sweeping changes in agricultural policy were politically important; the finance ministers asserted that the program would incur such large expenditures that they should have priority in the consultations; the agricultural ministers naturally believed that they should have most to say in a long-range plan calculated to change the face of agriculture in Western Europe. In addition to these intergovernmental and intragovernmental disputes, the program to reform agricultural structures caused frequent conflicts of interest between the various Community institutions: between the Commission and the Council of Ministers; in its early stages, between the individual members of the EEC Commission; and, finally, more controversy among local, regional, and national interest groups than there had ever been over any other Community proposal.

These multilevel, criss-crossing controversies provide one of the most fascinating and also one of the most complete cases for examining decisional processes in the European Community. In view of the complexity of the issue, and in order to avoid an imbalance with the other cases studied, it was decided to depart from the procedure followed up to date. Here, instead of following the case through all the preparatory stages from 1958, the details will be followed only from the launching of the Mansholt Plan in December 1968.

Image I: Financing Fights

The tug of war between foreign, agricultural, and finance ministers surfaced immediately. Although the French foreign minister, Mr. Debré insisted that the Commission inform the foreign ministers of the new agricultural proposals before it submitted them to the ministers of agriculture, EEC Commission Vice-President Mansholt outlined his proposals in December to a joint meeting of the foreign and agricultural ministers. Here too the question of French national interests was raised in no uncertain terms. Mr. Debré, the only minister to speak after Mr. Mansholt's comments on behalf of the EEC Commission, remarked acerbically: "The Commission's plan is only one working hypothesis. It in no way commits the national governments. France, for one, intends to submit proposals and it is only then that real negotiations between the Six will be embarked upon."[1] It was not too long before Mr. Debré's challenge found an answer. At the quarterly meeting of the ministers of finance held in Garmisch in January 1969, the German finance minister, Franz-Josef Strauss, stated bluntly: "Nationalizing advantages and making burdens a Community affair must not become a basic principle for the Community."[2] The finance ministers agreed that in future the probable cost of all Community farm policy decisions must be clearly estimated in advance so that the Council should have a clear picture of the financial implications of its decisions.

The cost of the agricultural reform program was the chief concern the first time the agricultural ministers met to consider the Mansholt Plan, in mid-January 1969. Although the meeting did not produce any sharp clashes, national alignments started to emerge. France lined up on the side of the EEC Commission and wanted the prices debate to be linked with the restructuring discussions, at least in the early stages. In the opposite camp, Germany and the Netherlands felt that the debate on prices should be given priority treatment, and structural reforms dealt with at some later date. This was a rather obvious attempt by Bonn and The Hague to get around the structural reform problem. Their final goal was the same, but their reasons were very different. The Dutch had been engaged in structural reform programs of their own for some considerable time and had no particular desire to subsidize other countries' plans in the area. Germany, on the other hand, was extremely sensitive about any project that implied some collectivization of the means of production.

With these major differences in outlook, the ministers of foreign affairs, finance, and agriculture of the Six met together in Brussels at the end of January 1969 to have their first general discussion of the Mansholt Plan. The debate became quite heated. Mr. Debré, vigorously defended France's insistence on more reciprocity in farm support from its partners, particularly from Germany. The French minister's approach had a somewhat inflammatory effect on the German delegation, which claimed that any cuts in food imports would lead to German market losses for its industrial exports.[3] Almost all the member states stressed the need to maintain considerable national autonomy. Quite clearly there was a close link between this issue and the financial problem in agriculture. If Community action was to be limited to the coordination of national programs, the governments would merely consult on the optimum size of holdings, and expenditures would be national. Some delegations took full advantage of the joint ministerial nature of the Council to stress their views in statements by two and even all three ministers.[4]

It is hardly surprising that the Council had to engage in some hard bargaining before it could work out an acceptable procedure for examining the Mansholt Plan and defining the spheres of competence of the agricultural, foreign, and finance ministers within the Council framework. It was decided that the prices for the coming season should be fixed as quickly as possible and before the structural policy was defined. These price decisions would be taken in the agricultural council. The problem of general price policy and that of agricultural surpluses would also be dealt with by the agricultural council. However, each of the member states could ask for these problems to be included at any time on the agenda of a general, i.e., foreign ministers council session. Structural, economic, social, financial, and trade problems would be discussed by the General Council.

This distribution of responsibilities was not an easy task for the Council in view of the extreme sensitivities of a number of the member states. Even at the preparatory level, national susceptibilities and intraministerial rivalries had to be taken into consideration. Preparation of meetings dealing with prices for the coming season was assigned to the Special Committee on Agriculture. The committee was to be assisted by financial experts and experts on trade policy. This system was also to apply to the preparation of agricultural council meetings on price policy and surpluses. In cases where a member state requested that an item be dealt with at a General Council, this item would be prepared by the Committee of Permanent Representatives. The General Council meetings dealing with structural, economic, social, financial, and trade problems would be prepared by the Committee of Permanent Representatives, who would be assisted by financial and trade experts. General Council meetings dealing with more technical agricultural questions would be prepared by the Special Committee on Agriculture.

It should be noted that participation of financial experts in all the work was a direct response to pressure from the finance ministers. The inclusion of trade policy experts in the preparation of decisions was made at the special request of Germany and the Netherlands in order to allay their anxieties over trade with nonmember countries.[5]

Despite this initial attempt by the ministers to take national sensitivities into consideration, the fundamental differences between the member countries came increasingly into the open as 1969 progressed. In March it was announced that the German ministry of agriculture was preparing a counterplan to be presented to the Council of Ministers the next time the Mansholt Memorandum came up for discussion. Had the German government not offered any alternative to the Mansholt idea of speeding up the rural exodus, it would have meant political suicide in an election year. All the German political parties were extremely hostile to the Mansholt Plan. In fact, the coalition government had already been under fire for some time from its Free Democrat and Socialist opponents for sacrificing German agriculture to the EEC.[6]

The German plan was published in June under the title "The Mansholt Plan—Criticisms and Alternatives," with a preface signed by the Federal agriculture minister, Mr. Hoecherl. The German government, while agreeing with the broad aims of the Mansholt Plan, accepted scarcely any of the measures proposed to implement it. It came out strongly in favor of limiting the quantities of products financially guaranteed by the Community and rejected for social (and, presumably, for electoral) reasons the proposed transformation in the size of holdings and the suggested numbers of farmers to leave the land by 1980, while advocating a "gradual evolution" and broad autonomy to carry out its own plans.[7] Less than two weeks later, the Federal finance minister, Franz-Josef Strauss, in a speech to a meeting of German farmers in Mainz, put the issue even more strongly. "We are not prepared to pay for ill-disguised patching up on the pretext of pursuing a European farm structures policy. From the financial point of view the Mansholt Plan is just not tenable." Later he said, "We will be hard put to find any way of channeling funds made available by the produce market support policy into the improvement of German farm structures."[8]

Not all the member states saw such clear disadvantages in the Mansholt proposals. France requested in May that a structural and social policy be achieved which would modify production conditions and improve farmers' living standards. Taking up Mr. Mansholt's idea, agriculture minister Boulin claimed that price mechanisms were not sufficient to attain the aims set out in the Rome Treaty. Mr. Mansholt interpreted this French statement as the first formal stand by a member state in favor of the general guidelines of the Commission's plans and expressed considerable satisfaction with it.[9]

The Dutch government also adopted a broadly positive approach to the Mansholt Plan later in 1969. In the so-called Lardinois Note, which contained the Dutch government's views on the EEC Commission's memorandum and which was submitted for approval to the upper house of the Dutch parliament along with the agricultural budget for 1970, the Dutch government maintained that it was "determined to make its contribution to the severe test which the common agricultural policy must face up to, wishing to keep in touch with reality but at the same time inspired by a constructive will toward the development of the common agricultural policy."[10] However, it did criticize some features of the Mansholt Plan quite strongly. It maintained that the link established by the Commission between structural reforms and the restoration of a market equilibrium was overly rigid. An effective price and market policy, it claimed, was still the best means of bringing about this equilibrium. There was also quite strong criticism of the Mansholt Plan's stress on large production units and large producers' groups.

Differences among the member countries were so sharp that when the EEC Commission submitted the first set of proposals to put the plan into effect to the Council in May 1970, big changes had been made. The proposals were framed in the form of directives, a procedure that highlighted the responsibility of the member states. (Under a Community directive, the member states themselves would choose the most appropriate action, thus limiting action to specific regions or varying it from one region to another. Use of the directives also meant that political debates would take place in the national parliaments when implementing legislation was enacted rather than at the Community level.) The "Mini-Mansholt Plan" thus completely dropped the idea of overall arrangements for the entire Community and picked up the notion that local situations and individual regional characteristics had to be taken into account, a point strongly urged by the Dutch and the Germans since the launching of the 1968 plan. Also in response to German pressure, the idea of a requisite size for farms was abandoned. The criterion finally adopted was that of aiding farms capable of reaching a certain minimum level of viability within a short time.[11] The German attitude was extremely disturbing to Commissioner Mansholt. On one occasion early in 1970 the German secretary of state for economic affairs declared that the West German taxpayer could not be expected to finance indefinitely structural improvements in other countries of the Community. Mr. Mansholt rejoined that for a government of socialists and free democrats, this was a very conservative and reactionary attitude.[12] As he was himself a socialist, this must have been particularly difficult to accept.

As 1970 progressed, a sense of impending crisis hung over the agricultural reforms. Mr. Mansholt pointed out that there could be no price proposals without complementary social and structural measures. Germany and the Netherlands, however, were interested in higher prices for their increasingly restive farmers. On the other side, the Italians would not approve any price increases without accompanying structural reforms. Since the Italians had no national programs for reform, and farms in Italy of less than 25 acres accounted for 40 percent of the total farming area and nearly nine-tenths of the number of holdings in the country, it was clearly in Italian interests to uphold Community-financed reforms and to oppose price increases. The French government also favored Community participation in reform but took a more independent line on prices. The Belgian government tended to support the French on this issue.

By the December 1970 Council meeting, the price situation had become so tense that the Dutch minister of agriculture, Pierre Lardinois, declared: "If there is no solution in the field of prices, then individual governments will have to take national measures."[13] Even an ultraprivate meeting of the ministers of agriculture in mid-December failed to iron out the fundamental differences of opinion. With a background of mounting unrest in poor farming communities, the agriculture ministers met in Brussels on February 15-16, 1971 to discuss what almost amounted to an EEC Commission ultimatum: any country that wanted price increases, however small, must also support reforms of the basic structure of farming.

It took the Council another month of hard bargaining, however, before any decision was reached on the prices-structures linkage. At the mid-February meeting no agreement was reached. Faced with a rapidly approaching April 1 deadline, the Council asked both the Committee of Permanent Representatives and the Special Committee on Agriculture to prepare the March 8-9 Council session. The Permanent Representatives were assigned to deal with the financial impact of the sociostructural measures and the Special Committee was asked to prepare the price mechanisms discussion. Nevertheless, the eager preparatory activities apparently masked considerable skepticism about the possibility of reaching an agreement. The German agriculture minister, Mr. Ertl, and his Italian counterpart, Mr. Natali, clashed on a number of occasions. The French and Belgians adopted a midway position and called for a policy commitment on structural reform. The Dutch preoccupations were mainly financial, in view of the advanced state of agricultural modernization in the Netherlands.[14]

German hostility to the EEC Commission's proposed link between prices and structures led to the submission of a counterproposal at the March 9 Council meeting. It was suggested that a link should be made between the reform of farm structures and the achievement of an economic and monetary union in the European Community. The new German plan aroused a measure of enthusiasm in some Community circles, particularly from the French government, which declared itself "interested" in the proposals.[15] But the Italians were adamant. In a speech on March 14 at the International Agricultural Fair in Verona, the Italian prime minister himself, Mr. Colombo, said:

One fact which has been prejudical to the whole of the achievement of the common agricultural policy is that market and pricing policy has not been coupled, as Italy requested, with a vigorous policy for overhauling the agricultural structures of the Community. . . . There has been a tendency on the part of many governments to take quick decisions about prices and to put off decisions regarding structures. . . . It would be wrong to imagine that the task of improving and stabilizing the incomes of the producers is a matter for the structures policy alone, but it is also emphasized . . . that a prices policy alone cannot ensure comparable benefits for all the farmers. . . . A prices policy which left a policy for structures on one side would be an illusory guarantee of a lower-cost common agricultural policy. . . . The Italian Government ought therefore to express its firm conviction that the prices policy and the Community policy for structures must be dovetailed and that this idea must be accepted both in practical terms and at the institutional level.[16]

Despite careful and lengthy preparations before the March 22-25 Council meeting in both the Special Committee on Agriculture and in the Permanent Representatives Committee, and a very slight softening in the positions adopted by some of the delegations, it did not look as if the ministers were going to find a way out of the prices-structures deadlock. The Council claimed that it intended to continue working until an overall agreement was reached. But for this to be possible, the various national viewpoints had first to move close enough together for some hope of compromise. Then a package deal would have to be worked out.

Late in the morning of March 25, after forty-five hours of fierce discussion, the ministers of agriculture emerged from the Council session with the first general agreement on the modernization of agricultural structures and a series of price increases for the 1971-72 season. According to observers, the delegations and EEC Commission members present were worn out when they left the conference room. The debate had gone badly until late the previous evening. Throughout the night of the twenty-fourth one compromise procedure after another was tried on the question of Community participation in financing. The negotiating tactic of isolating in turn the Italian delegation and the EEC Commission was used with some effectiveness. "At about 7:00 a.m.," to quote one observer, "the chances of success seemed to be increasingly smaller and the discussions continued in mediocrity, with purely national interests still prevailing. It was only at about 8:00 a.m. that . . . the stands of the various delegations began to become more flexible and an agreement was reached in the end on a new test."[17] The March 22-25, 1971 agricultural marathon was the longest in the history of the European Community. Circles close to the Common Market headquarters expressed their satisfaction with the results when the ministers emerged, but the battle of the conference table had apparently been unusually rough.

Image II: The Agricultural Organizations Turn the Screw

The EEC Commission, in its December 1968 memorandum, expressed the hope that its proposals would be widely discussed in all quarters, official and nonofficial. The memorandum's wide-ranging recommendations soon made it a topic of lively disucssion throughout the European Community. For some time public opinion had been prepared for a sharp change in direction in the common agricultural policy. Nevertheless, publication of the memorandum and press conference given by Commissioner Mansholt after its publication caused a sensation. Public reaction to the proposals ranged widely, from complete acceptance to total rejection. This second examination of the agricultural structures/prices decision endeavors to assess the influence brought to bear by the public and its representative bodies on agricultural decisional processes in the EEC between December 1968 and March 1971.

All groups in the Community were aware that a solution had to be found to the problems raised by the high cost of the common agricultural policy. There was also no doubt that agricultural structures required modernization. In a general way, therefore, both the opponents and defenders of the Mansholt program were in agreement on one vital point: previous Community policies had led nowhere, so it was vital to rethink the entire agricultural policy. This is one reason why the Mansholt Plan, even when most strongly criticized, was very rarely rejected in its entirety.

The immediate reactions were somewhat skeptical. Among nonagricultural groups, it was the long-term measures and financing problems that aroused attention. Among farmers and farm organizations, the chief concern was maintaining current income levels. Reactions also varied from country to country. The most positive came from the Netherlands and France. Italy apparently viewed the proposals with a certain amount of calm. In Belgium, there was a degree of hostility to reform of farm structures. It was among German farm groups, above all, that there were violent reactions. The target of their anger was the proposal to amalgamate holdings.

Reactions to the Proposed Reforms

The Commission's proposal to reduce the prices of certain agricultural commodities provoked negative reactions in many quarters. In an article in the *Süddeutsche Zeitung*, Mr. Mansholt was accused of pushing as many farmers as possible to leave the farm by means of "systematic demoralization" and a massive reduction of prices.[18] In the Netherlands, the president of the farmers' organizations, Mr. Knotterus, claimed that the proposals were both disappointing and mostly unacceptable. "I believe," he said, "that Mr. Mansholt is so impressed by the financial repercussions of the existence of surpluses that he wants to reduce them by the price policy."

The French chambers of agriculture also came out against any price reduction or stabilization. Almost all the other French farmers' organizations objected to proposed reductions in beef prices. The three Belgian farmers' organizations expressed particular surprise that the EEC Commission was proposing price reduction not only of surplus commodities but also of products like feed grains and beef where demand exceeded supply.[19]

Reactions to the structural proposals varied considerably. They were most positive among associations of young farmers and fairly good among food trade and food processing organizations. In contrast, farmers' groups in Germany, particularly in Bavaria and the south, were violently hostile to the proposals. As *Le Monde* commented, Germans found the suggestion of forming large holdings of a collective nature totally unacceptable psychologically. This inevitably reminded them of the East German cooperatives.[20] It is hardly surprising, therefore, that Mr. von Feury, the president of the Bavarian Peasants' League, claimed that Mr. Mansholt was proposing "cold-blooded socialization," the formation of "volunteers' *kolkhozes*." Von Feury demanded the EEC commissioner's resignation.[21] Belgian farmers were also afraid that family farms would disappear and adopted a rather negative attitude. The food industry in Belgium, on the other hand, was not hostile to the plans for restructuring farms. In an era of large corporations and industrial mergers, it was difficult to see how small family farms could continue to exist. In the neighboring Netherlands, the need to modernize farm structures was much easier to accept. The aims seemed to be realistic and necessary. It was the financial implications of the restructuring that particularly worried the Dutch. Almost the entire Dutch press commented adversely on the financial inadequacies of the plan.[22]

The two major farm organizations in Italy, the Coltivatori Diretti, a Christian Democrat organization representing more than three million farmers, and the Confagricoltura, a Liberal organization representing large landholders, both came out in favor of structural reforms. The various left-wing organizations, on the other hand, claimed that the Mansholt Plan was attempting to "liquidate the small farmer."[23] Italian employers' organizations were more moderate in their reactions. They adopted the attitude that the Mansholt Plan had deliberately engaged in shock tactics and that it was better to deal with structural reforms according to the specific needs of each country.[24]

Reactions in France ranged from the almost unequivocal support of the Centre national des jeunes agriculteurs to the criticism of the Fédération nationale de la propriété agricole, which condemned Mr. Mansholt's desire "to impose a theoretical model of farming when experience shows that it is out of date even before it has seen the light of day."[25] Between the two came a voice of caution from Mr. Duclos of the Fédération nationale des syndicats d'exploitants agricoles (FNSEA): "Do not forget," he said, "that systematic opposition from us could lead the states to allow this change to take place by natural means and that would be much more serious."[26]

Organizational Attitudes

During the course of 1969, the European-level organizations issued opinions on the Mansholt Memorandum. The Comité des organisations professionelles agricoles (COPA), which groups all the national farming organizations in the EEC, made known its views in March. The doubts already expressed by farmers throughout the European Community were reiterated by the COPA's president, Mr. Jean Deleau. A major point of criticism was that the Mansholt Plan did not include any overall trade plan for agricultural products, despite suggestions made by the EEC Commission during the Kennedy Round negotiations that there should be world commodity agreements. The COPA was strongly critical of the EEC Commission for being less willing than some countries, the United States for example, to protect its traditional markets. Further strong criticism was voiced by the COPA of alleged overoptimism about the number of farmers scheduled to leave the land and be reemployed elsewhere.[27]

In October the Union des industries de la Communauté Européenne (UNICE) published its opinion on the EEC Commission's memorandum. The opinion dealt in turn with policies on agricultural markets, financing, trade, improving agricultural structures, and the social aspects of agricultural reform. In some respects, UNICE was highly critical of the EEC Commission. Agricultural policy in the Community, it was asserted, had been pursued too one-sidedly, and macroeconomic considerations had not been taken sufficiently into consideration. UNICE criticized the Mansholt Plan for not giving definite details on the cost of the measures it advocated. Regrets were also expressed that the Commission's proposals had barely touched on problems of trade policy. As far as improving agricultural structures, however, UNICE supported the Commission's view that this should be part of an economic and social policy based on general economic considerations. The organization maintained that such large-scale reforms could not be carried out simply within the framework of a customs union coupled with a common agricultural policy. The Commission's reform proposals, it declared, were a step in the right direction and should be used as a means of developing and consolidating the European Community.[28]

Very shortly after the UNICE statement, the Executive Committee of the European Federation of Free Trade Unions in the EEC and the Executive Board of the European Organization of the World Confederation of

Labor (Christian unions) came out with a joint policy statement on the EEC Commission's "Memorandum 1980." The two trade union organizations regarded the overhaul of agriculture as a matter of great urgency. They urged that the reform should not impair the living and working security of the farmers concerned and that it take more account of the interests of consumers. The Commission's view that larger farms were needed to improve production structures was supported by the unions, although the definitions of "production unit" and "modern farm" were not considered sufficiently flexible. The unions were opposed to any discrimination in the allocation of social assistance. "Such assistance," they asserted, "should be the same for workers, owners, farmers and managers." They wanted to see an appreciable cut in the prices of all products affected by the imbalances in the market and to see the producers bear a share of the cost of surpluses. The unions agreed with the EEC Commission that the emphasis placed on supporting prices and markets should be shifted as soon as possible to a structural policy.[29]

Despite labor union and EEC Commission eagerness to shift the emphasis away from prices, events at the end of 1969, above all the revaluation of the German mark and the subsequent loss of income for German farmers, led to an extremely tense situation. German farm organizations were very critical of the Mansholt proposals. In a letter to the press early in 1970, Mr. Rehwinkel, a former president of the German Bauernverband, stated that larger farms would not mean an appreciable improvement in farmers' incomes if wages and prices of industrial goods and services continued rise. He went on to accuse Mr. Mansholt in very strong terms of having failed to make his own economic concepts prevail against the sectionalism of the member countries. "You should draw the obvious consequences and resign," he concluded.[30]

In March 1970 the results of a survey conducted among German farmers bore out Mr. Rehwinkel's comments. On the whole, the survey indicated, German farmers were dissatisfied with the EEC and considered that their interests were inadequately represented in Brussels. More than half the farmers questioned would rather have had increased prices than direct state subsidies. Fifty-seven percent of those questioned were against a policy of establishing large industrial-style farms.[31] The Bauernverband took the issue up in April and published a motion calling for the abolition of the Community farm price system, which it considered too rigid.[32]

Discontent over Community price policy was not restricted to German farmers. In the Netherlands also farmers began to make their feelings known in the spring of 1970. In Frisia, Mr. Lardinois, the minister of agriculture, was beseiged by about 1500 angry farmers in the hotel where he was having talks with the leaders of the agricultural unions, and the police had to intervene. The farmers were primarily concerned about the prices of milk and dairy products, which they claimed were moving more and more out of line with real production costs. A few days later, organizations of fruit producers in the Netherlands gave the Dutch government a two-week ultimatum to find a solution for the difficulties in the fruit and vegetables sector.[33]

It was against this background of widespread reaction, criticism, and comment that, at the end of April 1970, the EEC Commission introduced its modified proposals for the reform of agriculture, the so-called Mini-Mansholt Plan. It is interesting to note the extent to which the new, modified plan responded to what Commissioner Mansholt had described as one of the prime aims of the 1968 proposals: to present deliberately stark options in order to provoke widespread public discussion; to prompt thorough debate in all the Community bodies and in the economic and social organs of the six member states. The EEC Commission claimed that, after receiving all the reactions, criticisms, encouragements and reservations, it had been able to take them into account, modify some lines, make others more flexible, and translate the principles of the plan into projects to be implemented.

The new proposals had clearly not revamped the 1968 plan sufficiently to silence farmers' criticism throughout the Community. In France, the Fédération nationale des syndicats d'exploitants agricoles français (FNSEA) vigorously criticized the new proposals put forward by Mr. Mansholt. It totally rejected the idea that subsidies should be limited to a relatively small number of Community farmers. There could be no question, the FNSEA said, of blocking the development of a large number of family farms from the outset. Adoption of measures of this kind, it threatened, might lead farmers to withdraw their support from European policy.[34]

Support for the EEC Commission's policy began to be withdrawn in the second half of 1970. At the annual general meeting of the COPA in June, the delegates, in the presence of growing farmers' discontent, called upon the COPA to make vigorous representations to the Community bodies in order to ensure that when agricultural prices were fixed for the 1971-72 season, the "intolerable process of erosion of the farmers' living conditions" would be reversed.[35] In October 1970, Mr. Jean Deleau, the COPA's president, demanded general increases in farm prices. The Community authorities in Brussels, he said, had underestimated farmers' discontent. Community prices, he alleged, were badly directed because of political compromises. The president of the Belgian Boerenbond, Mr. Boon, made an even more aggressive statement over Belgian radio. In the past, Mr. Boon claimed, the EEC Commission had created an "overproduction psychosis." In this way they had prevented farmers from obtaining price increases by depicting surplus production as more serious than it actually was. "It was itself a significant result," Mr. Boon asserted, "to have prevented the price reductions suggested by the Commission by means of political pressure." The Commission's position, which, he said, was one of not proposing new prices until the Council came up with a decision on the structural proposals, was unacceptable.[36]

By January 1971, farmers' groups throughout the Community were preparing to swing into action against what they considered to be inadequate price proposals by the EEC Commission. About 15,000 Belgian farmers in the Liège area threatened to organize demonstrations against the alleged disparity between farmers' incomes and those of other workers.[37] A week later, the COPA announced that it would hold a special general assembly in Brussels on March 23, when the Council of Ministers was scheduled to decide on Commodity prices for the coming season. The COPA announced that it wanted to demonstrate in this way the presence of farmers and their concern over deteriorating incomes. In February, the French national farmers' federation came out against the EEC Commission's link between price proposals and structural reforms.

Given the present inflationary situation and the appalling way European agricultural prices have stayed static for years, decisions on these lines would produce very sharp reactions among French country people. A substantial upvaluing of prices is essential to the increase in agricultural earnings that is so abundantly justified by the trend in earnings elsewhere.[38]

Agricultural organizations throughout the Community warned of the consequences if the EEC Commission and the Council of Ministers did not produce some satisfactory solution to the prices/structures problem. Scarcely had the meeting of the agricultural council opened on February 15, when about a hundred Belgian farmers burst into the room. The farmers brought with them a number of cows. The demonstrators demanded a rise in farm prices, a reform of structures, and chanted slogans hostile to the Council and to Mr. Mansholt for about half an hour before they were induced to leave.[39]

From the mid-February Council meeting until the end of the March 23-25 marathon, the farmers' organizations did not relax their pressure. In Germany and France, large-scale demonstrations were planned. In Belgium the EEC Commission and the common agricultural policy were vigorously attacked.[40] The entire morning prior to the March 8 session of the agricultural council was taken up by a meeting between the council president, Mr. Cointat, and members of the COPA.[41] During the week before the March 23-25 marathon, announcement followed announcement from the organizations about their plans. It soon became clear that official reassurances about the size and peacefulness of the farmers' demonstrations were unlikely to be borne out. The Belgian organizations stated that a parade would be held through the center of Brussels to protest the EEC Commission's price proposals. A couple of days later, the president of the COPA, Mr. Vetrone, sent a telegram to the ministers of agriculture which stated once again that the COPA could not accept the Commission's price proposals because they failed to ensure an immediate improvement on farmers' incomes.[42]

The quiet demonstration announced by the agricultural organizations for March 23 turned into a violent protest in which approximately 80,000 Western European farmers swarmed through Brussels, demanding increased prices for their produce. Automobiles were burned, street signs were torn up, and windows broken. During the demonstration, one man was killed and 140 persons were injured. The demonstration, which assumed riot proportions, attracted farmers from all the member countries of the Common Market. They carried heavy wooden pitchforks and swept down the main Boulevard Anspach twenty abreast despite the presence of three thousand police brought out to control the demonstrators. The Brussels demonstration marked the peak of a week of separate protests in the various member countries. In Germany and Eastern Belgium farmers blocked the roads. Flemish farmers sent the Belgian vice-premier, André Cools, seven thousand packages of potatoes in the mail to protest that their earnings were not keeping up with the cost of living. In France, peasants demonstrated in the northern and central regions. They broke windows of police stations and blocked road and rail traffic in Brittany and Normandy.

While the farmers were demonstrating in the center of Brussels, the ministers of the Six were meeting in the Council headquarters behind a protective barrier of concertina wire, water cannon, and heavily armed police. On the same day, the special assembly of the COPA brought together about 1,200 leaders of agricultural organizations in the Palais des Congrès (the usual meeting place of the Council of Ministers of the Community) during the morning. After several hours of discussion, the meeting voted a resolution that was submitted to the president of the EEC Council of Ministers, Mr. Cointat, and to Mr. Malfatti, president of the Commission of the European Communities. The COPA expressed the "discouragement and disappointment of Community farmers in face of the immobilism of the common agricultural policy." As the "interpretor of the unanimous will of European farmers," it declared that the "constant deterioration in the situation of Community agriculture seriously compromises the future of the EEC." The special general assembly called the EEC Commission's price proposals "absolutely inadequate and incomplete." Finally, the COPA brought out the heavy guns:

The Extraordinary General Assembly solemnly warns the Council against the current immobilism of the common agricultural policy. Only an active and dynamic policy can give farmers, particularly young farmers, confidence in the Community and avoid the collapse of the common agricultural policy. Without suitable Community measures, the necessary national measures to solve the problems of farmers' incomes will certainly not fail to be taken, thus dangerously compromising the unity of the Community.[43]

After the voting of the resolution, the Executive Committee of the COPA was closeted for several hours during the afternoon of March 23 with Mr. Cointat, Mr. Malfatti, and Mr. Mansholt. The leaders of the EEC institutions assured the COPA that its views would be taken into consideration and that a decision was hoped for the same evening. The Council of Ministers did not reach its final decisions until almost two days later. The farmers got price rises—the first since April 1, 1968. Admittedly they did not get the 10 percent that they had demanded, but they did obtain some measure of satisfaction. As one political commentator remarked shortly after the demonstration:

It has taken the farmers several years to realize they no longer can influence common prices by demonstrating nationally. When they came to Brussels—almost every farmer in Belgium came, but so did thousands from France, Italy, Germany, and the Netherlands—it showed that this shift to the European level had become a political reality.[44]

The close connection between the farmers' riots and the Council's concessions seems to indicate a strong correlation between public pressure and Community action in this instance. The connection between persistent pressure from some of the strongest organizational groups in the Community and Mr. Mansholt's determination to submit compromise packages for consideration by the Council of Ministers also points clearly to the ability of the farmers and the groups, when they were sufficiently determined and pushed hard enough, to move the EEC Commission. According to all reports, Mr. Mansholt was profoundly shaken by the magnitude and the violence of the Brussels demonstrations. The attacks on Mr. Mansholt were extremely personal and this played a significant part in the commissioner's determination to engineer the compromise decision of March 25. The demonstrations undoubtedly marked a crisis in the history of the European Community which, according to many EEC officials, left a deep scar.[45]

Image III: The Mansholt Mystique

When the March 1971 structures/prices decision is viewed through the elite networks lens, one is very forcibly struck by the towering position occupied throughout by Sicco Mansholt. The loyalties and antagonisms he aroused, his relationships with his colleagues in the EEC Commission, his dealings with members of the national governments, the farmers' organizations, and the general public are all marked by his personality. This emerges both from the printed record and from interviews. He was described by one of his aides as a "man difficult to withstand. But for his drive and conviction, the whole agricultural policy would not be what it is today." The same aide commented: "Certainly if another commissioner had been in charge of agriculture, policy in that area would have been quite different, particularly as far as structures are concerned, as there is very little provision made for it in the Rome Treaty."[46]

From the very beginning, as an official of the Economic and Social Committee of the European Communities pointed out, Mr. Mansholt wanted to run the Community's agricultural policy.[47] This is borne out by an EEC Commission document from as far back as April 1959. "We are aware," it begins, "that the common agricultural policy must be concerned both with agricultural structures and with markets. Mr. Mansholt's idea is to completely modernize these structures within the space of a generation."[48]

There are two remarkable features about this document. Not only does it talk about modernizing agricultural structures in almost the same terms as eight or nine years later; it specifically mentions Mr. Mansholt by name (an unusual feature in EEC documents) as the originator of the idea. Commissioner Mansholt also prepared the ground with great political care. As a socialist of European reputation, he knew that he would run into considerable suspicion and difficulties in some of the member countries, particularly in traditionally conservative French agricultural circles. In order to counter this, Mansholt included on his staff for some years a French official whose prime task was to convince the organizations in the member countries that the Commission's agricultural policies were not too aggressively socialist. By skillful maneuvering, Mr. Mansholt came to a kind of gentleman's agreement with the French: he would help them in the agricultural sector so long as they did not present too much opposition to certain aspects of his policies likely to be interpreted as socialist. This kind of bargaining, as one official pointed out, was a constant in Mr. Mansholt's politics from the very beginning. He also surrounded himself by extremely able and loyal aides, chief of whom was Alfred Mozer, a Dutchman well known in European circles.

The force of Sicco Mansholt's personality extended far beyond his immediate aides into other areas of the European Community bureaucracy and seems to have affected almost everyone with whom he came into contact. As an aide pointed out: "He was the only member of the EEC Commission known on a Community-wide basis, the only name known way beyond agricultural circles right down to the uninformed."[49] An EEC Commission official told the story of a meeting at which Mr. Mansholt was scheduled to appear in France. "We had heard that there had been threats made against him and we tried to persuade him not to go," he said. "He insisted on going, and when he got up to speak he said: 'I have heard that you want to kill me, but listen to me first' and after half an hour they applauded him."[50] Coincidentally, as the story was being told, the commissioner himself walked across the main hallway of the EEC headquarters building. The official pointed him out and the note of admiration that came into the voice of a man who had worked in fairly close contact with Mr. Mansholt for more than ten years was telling evidence of the respect with which he was held by colleagues and associates.

This kind of influence stemmed not only from personality; it was also carefully studied. One official from outside the EEC Commission told of the way in which interpreters are frequently blamed by government and EEC officials for misunderstandings at meetings. "Mansholt," he said, "has always defended the interpreters. He has a reputation for this and it is a very important factor in a multilingual organization."[51] It is hardly surprising that a humane, understanding official of the highest rank aroused enthusiasm among his own staff, since these are qualities rarely found to such a degree among bureaucrats in Mr. Mansholt's position. Even more surprising, these feelings were expressed even by the press. The *Financial Times* of London commented in May 1970:

It can't be too strongly emphasized that in many respects the acceptance of the Common Agricultural Policy so far has been due to the strength of Mansholt's personality. He is an impressive, very dignified character, speaks with complete assurance, and great fluency and is supported by a loyal staff who treat any suggestions of change with about as much enthusiasm as that with which the Pope welcomes birth control or the marriage of the clergy.[52]

With this description of Mr. Mansholt as a backdrop, it is illuminating to follow his activities and his dealings with ministers, members of the EEC Commission, and representatives of farmers' organizations on the European, national, and local levels from the launching of the Mansholt Plan in December 1968 until the March 1971 Council marathon.

Even before the plan was publicly announced, Mr. Mansholt had to contend with opposition from two sides. On the one hand, within the EEC Commission itself some members wondered whether it was really necessary or, for that matter, possible to have the Community finance the entire costly undertaking of modernizing the farm sector in the name of industrial society's historic debt to agriculture. Ranged against Mr. Mansholt and his idea of a planned and subsidized "liquidation" of the existing system were the German and Italian commissioners, headed by Mr. von der Groeben. Mr. Mansholt also had to contend with opposition from the Council of Ministers, particularly from the French foreign minister, Michel Debré.

The six member governments were markedly suspicious of what was regarded as a resurgence of EEC Commission power. In the absence of complete agreement on the agricultural proposals within the Commission, Mr. Mansholt would have been obliged to present to the Council of Ministers a plan for which he undertook personal commitment. Mr. Debré was fully aware of this. In a series of skirmishes with the Commission, the French minister bitterly attacked the Mansholt Plan and labeled it merely "one working document among others." He then asked the Commission as a whole to present detailed texts to the Council as soon as possible. This move by Mr. Debré was interpreted in Brussels as expressly intended to get Mr. Mansholt into difficulties. It was asserted that the French minister, by forcing the EEC Commission to reach a hasty compromise, was attempting to prove that the Commission was not equipped to play the political role that it sought. It was also considered to be a personal response to Mr. Mansholt, who was suspected of wanting to show that the Commission alone was able to propose an effective solution to the farm problem. It would thus take the lead over the national governments, who were allegedly prisoners of their farm electorates. Mr. Mansholt adroitly avoided these pitfalls by persuading the Commission to agree a week later on the text it was to submit to the Council.[53] Mr. Mansholt's responsibility for the proposed structural reforms was also challenged by Mr. Höcherl, the Federal Republic's minister of agriculture. On December 11, he pointed out that the proposals represented Mr. Mansholt's personal views and not a European Commission decision.[54] However, the EEC Commission president, Jean Rey, gave Mr. Mansholt his full backing.

From January 1969 on, Commissioner Mansholt and a small team of aides embarked on a wide-ranging publicity campaign for their plan. Initially, the enterprise seemed hopeless. The protagonists were up against traditionalism and conservatism on both the right and the left. Early in January, Mr. Mansholt appeared on French television with four leaders of French farm organizations: Mr. Gérard de Caffarelli of the FNSEA, Mr. René Blondelle of the Chambres d'agriculture, Mr. Michel Simon of the Jeunes agriculteurs, and Mr. Alfred Nègre of the Mouvement de défense des exploitants familiaux.[55] Before the month was out, Mr. Mansholt was in Rome speaking about his program at a convention of the Coltivatori Diretti.[56] Less than two weeks later he was in Berlin and vigorously defended his proposals at the annual Green Week.[57]

Month after month, Mr. Mansholt toured Europe and talked with ministers, farm organizations, and farm workers in the member countries. Slowly, the dialogue he set in motion from Brittany to Bavaria and from Flanders to Calabria started to pay off. Mr. Mansholt, true to style, concentrated much of his effort on the French scene and attempted to defuse the stiffest opposition there. In March he appeared at a large meeting in Lille with his fellow commissioner, Gaullist Raymond Barre, former French minister of agriculture Edgard Pisani, and the president of the French wheat producers' association, Jean Deleau (also newly elected president of the COPA).[58] In June he went to Auvergne in central France to speak to farmers there, and in July he addressed one of the most hostile groups of all, the Fédération des exploitants de l'ouest in Nantes. This group, led by Mr. Bernard Lambert, had been a perpetual thorn in the side of the Commission since 1962. But instead of rejecting the Mansholt proposals, the Nantes group submitted a series of constructive criticisms.[59] While Mr. Mansholt had, for example, faced hostile demonstrations from the audience in Kiel in December, for the most part, the vice-president of the EEC Commission was able to bring the local and regional groupings of farmers partially around to his way of thinking during the course of 1969.

Despite his enormous personal influence, there seems to be little doubt that Mr. Mansholt would not have been able to make the progress he made in 1969 and early 1970 without the network of contacts that had been built up over the years between the EEC Commission and the farm organizations. This was particularly true of contacts between the COPA and the EEC Commission and between certain national farm leaders and the EEC Commission. One official went as far as to label the farm organization leaders as the "agricultural mafia."[60]

In fact, there was already a fair amount of transnational contact between the various national farm groups even before the Common Market came into existence. From the time the COPA set up its secretariat in Brussels in April 1959, its officials met regularly with members of the EEC Commission and particularly with Mr. Mansholt. The executive committee of the COPA, composed of six representatives, one from each member country of the Community designated by the national organizations, usually their presidents, also met monthly with Commissioner Mansholt. In addition to this contact, many of the leaders of the farm organizations also met on a fairly regular basis in the Economic and Social Committee of the European Community. Some of them had been members from the inception of the Committee.

A picture thus begins to form of a group of men who knew each other very well indeed. As one official remarked: "When someone in the Commission gets up and says 'the COPA says such and such,' everyone knows what it means."[61] In this group were a number of men who were accustomed to playing a highly political role in their own countries and who led organizations that wielded considerable influence on the national scene. In Belgium, for example, the Belgische Boerenbond is not only a grouping of producers but a strong cooperative with interests in banks, feedstuff production, and distribution. Its president is automatically a member of the board of governors of the national bank. As one commentator put it: "All agricultural power is concentrated in Boon, the president of the Boeren-bond. In another interview, he said: "Whenever there is a major agricultural problem, to all intents and purposes the only phone call made by the Belgian expert or the Belgian minister is to Boon."[62]

In the Netherlands, the hub of the agricultural organization, which is extremely well-knit and exercises a strong influence on the government, is constituted of graduates of the Wageningen agricultural university. They all know each other, one Community official pointed out, in the organizations, in the Dutch Parliament, in the European Parliament, in the Economic and Social Committee.[63] The head of the Luxembourg farm organization, the Centrale paysanne luxembourgeoise, Mr. Berns, also played an extremely influential part in establishing and maintaining the network of European farm leaders and in enhancing their role as a highly influential pressure group comparable with the strongest lobby. While Luxembourg is small, the influence of Mr. Berns is felt throughout the Common Market and even beyond. He has developed and cultivated ties in Scandinavia and Britain, travels frequently to the United States, and, as one observer put it, has friends everywhere and is invited everywhere.[64] It is hardly surprising that when men like Berns and Boon got together and when the Dutch farm leaders mobilized their forces, they constituted a force at times difficult to resist.

It was partly because of the strength of these individual leaders, their ability to mobilize or demobilize their national following, and their personal ties with Mr. Mansholt and his close aides, that, by contrast, reactions to the March 23, 1971 demonstrations were so very bitter on all sides, so much so that Mr. Mansholt and Mr. Boon embarked on an acrimonious public fight. In an exchange of letters, Mr. Boon described Mr. Mansholt as a "caged rat snapping right and left." Mr. Mansholt, in turn, accused Mr. Boon of intemperance, irresponsibility, and lies.[65] It appears that Mr. Mansholt felt betrayed by a group of men whom he had learned to know extremely well and who had given him repeated assurances that the demonstrations they were organizing would be peaceful and orderly.

The leaders of the farm organizations, on the other hand, had their local constituencies to look to and their own internal politics to consider. In one television interview between Mr. Mansholt and a farm leader, there was a sharp disagreement between the two. Afterwards, according to a member of Mansholt's staff, the leader turned to Mr. Mansholt and said: "Of course I agree with you but I cannot say so in public."[66] Some of the farmers from the poorer regions were quite desperate in early 1971. They had experienced a bad winter, and March is traditionally a month where there is not a great deal of farm activity. Also, they had had all winter to brood about their unenviable situation and to compare their lot unfavorably with that of other workers. It was not unnatural that their leaders should look to Mr.

Mansholt and the EEC Commission for redress, and not unnatural that they should feel deceived and wronged when they did not obtain all they had been demanding.

The personal touch was also relied on very much when Mr. Mansholt dealt with the member governments. Throughout 1970 he encountered stiffening opposition to his proposals from the national authorities. They were even hostile to the modified "Mini-Mansholt Plan" of the spring of 1970, which gave the member states much more than the original 1968 proposals. Mr. Mansholt, somewhat encouraged by the results of his 1969 public relations campaign among the local and regional organizations, embarked on phase II of this campaign in the early autumn of 1970—a tour of the member capitals to meet with ministers and experts and consult on a bilateral level. At the September 29, 1970 meeting of the agricultural council, Mr. Mansholt announced his tour and went on to say that it would then be possible for the six ministers of agriculture and the EEC Commission to meet outside the framework of the Council for an informal gathering before the Commission submitted further proposals on structures and prices at the end of the year.[67]

The ministers had their informal meeting at the chateau of Val Duchesse in Brussels in December, but Mr. Mansholt did not let up his lobbying. In March 1971, faced with bitter opposition from the German farmers to the EEC Commission's proposal to link price decisions with structural reforms, Mr. Mansholt went to meet with the Federal chancellor, Willy Brandt. The meeting took place on a Sunday morning at the chancellor's private residence and was attended also by Mr. Ertl, the minister of agriculture, Mr. Genscher, the minister of the interior, Mr. von Braun, the secretary of state for foreign affairs, and Mr. Wehner, the leader of the socialist group in the German parliament. The proceedings were ultra-secret, but it was known that Mr. Mansholt was endeavoring to persuade the German authorities to soften a little their implacable position on the primacy of price increases over structural reforms.[68]

The price situation was such a problem at the March 23-25 Council marathon that there seemed a definite danger that the common farm policy would be split in two: unpopular price decisions would be taken in Brussels, and structural policy would remain national. Mr. Mansholt's triumph, on the day after the Brussels demonstrations, was to bring the Council of Ministers to accept an overall plan for the entire Community area. He achieved this by his skillful use of the leverage that an adroit Commission can exercise between countries. Italy, with the most severe structural problems, needed money from its partners to pay for the necessary changes. Without a Community settlement, there could be no agreement on prices, which would have meant more discontent in other countries of the Community. So, reluctantly, the ministers agreed to the Mansholt compromise proposals. As one press commentator pointed out: "If Europe's farming problem is solved by 1980 . . . it will be above all Mr. Mansholt's achievement."[69]

There seems to be no exception to the universal recognition of Mr. Mansholt's importance in shaping the agricultural decision of March 1971—from being hung in effigy by rioting farmers in the streets of Brussels to the inaugural statement of French minister of agriculture, Michel Cointat, as president of the Council in January 1971. Mr. Cointat, speaking of his high esteem for Mr. Mansholt and for his courageous action, went on to say: "Even if sometimes we have not always agreed, we must recognize as friends that without his will, agricultural Europe would not be where it is."[70]

The farm structures case has revealed some highly unusual elements in European Community decisional behavior. Never before had the Community witnessed such sustained public protest directed not at the member governments in the six national capitals but at the Community itself in Brussels. Never before had a member of the EEC Commission been associated personally with an idea for so long, nursing it from the time he entered the EEC Commission in 1958 until he consciously exploded it like a firecracker on the Community scene in December 1968. From the time the Mansholt Plan was made public and submitted to the Council of Ministers at the end of 1968 until the structural and price reform proposals were adopted in March 1971, commissioner Mansholt engaged in a public relations campaign on a scale never before seen in the European Community. He was subject to personal, at times vituperative, attacks more in keeping with attacks on a national political figure than a member of the European bureaucracy.

Probably the most striking feature to emerge from this three-lens study of the farm structures decision is the link between the three approaches formed by the presence of a distinct elite network in the first two images as well as in the third.

Socialization mechanisms seem to have manifested themselves and induced international coalition formation at different levels of the Community's decision-making system in agricultural issues. A sense of solidarity seems to have existed among ministers, farm organizations leaders, and European Community bureaucrats that far surpassed that in other issue areas. In none of the previous case studies has this link been so clear cut.

7 Economic and Monetary Union

Under the Rome Treaty, economic and monetary policies fall under the authority of the member states. But the treaty does recognize that economic and monetary actions in the individual member countries are interdependent. Consequently, when the European Community was set up, provision was made for the coordination of national policies in these areas. As the 1960s progressed, however, it became increasingly apparent that the coordination machinery installed in a rather piecemeal fashion was ineffective. By 1967-68, there was talk in Community circles of the need for closer and closer coordination. But not until late 1969 was the word *coordination* replaced by *union*. The monetary and economic union proposal was given the final stamp of approval at The Hague summit meeting in December 1969.

The idea of instituting a full economic and monetary union in the European Community, even though it was launched with considerable fanfare at the EEC summit meeting, was an enormous step in the dark for the six Community members. Economic and monetary affairs had fallen within the national preserve for so long. It is not surprising, therefore, that before the Council of Ministers took their decision in February 1971 to go ahead with setting up the union, there were constant battles in which national representatives pushed for policies aimed at promoting the economic and monetary well-being of their own countries. Also not surprising is the strong temptation to view the decision exclusively as the outcome of these battles.

Only when the events leading up to the decision are viewed from different standpoints does the decision emerge as a more complex process. From the standpoint of the interest groups and representative bodies, for example, the rapidity with which the decision was reached (only fifteen months elapsed between The Hague summit and the February 1971 Council decision) becomes more comprehensible. It was in the interest of employers and workers alike to give the proposals their backing. Hence, feelings in the national parliaments and in the European Parliament on the broad aims, if not on the details, of the proposals were not hostile.

When the decision is viewed through the elite networks lens, we see an extremely elaborate process. Many different but overlapping bodies had gradually been established to deal with economic and monetary affairs in the Community. These included the Council of Ministers, its semiofficial meetings of ministers of finance, its Monetary Committee, Short-Term Economic Policy Committee, Committee of Governors of Central Banks, Budget Policy Committee, Medium-Term Economic Policy Committee, and many small ad hoc groups. Outside the Community also, ministers of finance and economic affairs, governors of central banks, and economic and financial experts had been getting together regularly since the end of World War II at meetings of the International Monetary Fund, the World Bank, and OECD. The individuals in the EEC responsible for policy proposals and decisions on economic and monetary matters knew each other very well indeed by 1970.

Image I: The Economists Versus the Monetarists

Despite the general agreement at The Hague on the desirability of an economic and monetary union in the European Community, there were clearly sharp differences between the member states about the means of instituting such a union. From the beginning, there were two conflicting concepts: the economic and the monetary. The "economists" viewed the hasty forging of currency ties as excessively risky in view of the wide structural differences between the member countries. It was their view that currency integration without the previous harmonization of economic policies would be like building a house without foundations; the currency union would face the same constant danger of collapse. The "monetarists," on the other hand, aimed at forcing structural compatibility and economic harmonization by introducing currency ties as early as possible.

These differences of opinion about the correct method of instituting an economic and monetary union sprang both from different economic traditions and from deep-seated differences in political aims. The French particularly were extremely reluctant to commit themselves to the idea of an economic and monetary union that would possess "supranational" characteristics as, for example, some kind of new, central implementing body. This reluctance clearly steered them in the direction of a monetary rather than an economic union. The "economists," on the other hand, worked on the principle that a necessary harmonization of economic policies could not be achieved without an efficient, central Community authority to provide the structure for decison-making. For them, progress toward an economic union was synonymous with progress toward a political union in the Community. The Germans and the Dutch, frequently the proponents of increased supranationality, tended to stress the political need for an economic and monetary union. The divergent views emerge clearly from the public statements of government leaders from the six Community countries during the 1969-71 period.

The French minister of defense, Mr. Michel Debré, in an interview with a Paris weekly in January 1971, did not mince his words: "There is no such thing as monetary Europe," he said. "Europe is either political and has a currency or it does not exist and has no currency."[1] In April 1970, the Belgian minister of financial affairs, Baron Snoy et d'Oppuers, voiced a very similar opinion:

The introduction of a European monetary unit does not necessarily mean bringing in a European currency. . . . From a purely technical point of view both are equally valid arrangements but the creation of a European currency has more obvious political implications and would require a politically united Europe in which all the important decisions would be taken by a common authority.[2]

On the "economists" side, Mr. Schöllhorn, secretary of state at the German ministry of economic affairs, speaking on his return from the June 1970 conference of the EEC ministers of finance and economic affairs in Venice, said that the Federal government was more interested in correlating monetary and short-term economic integration in a practical way than in hasty monetary decisions.[3] After October 1970, when the Werner Plan was made public, German governmental authorities continued to stress overall parallelism between economic and monetary union and short-term priority for the harmonization of economic policies. Mr. Karl Schiller, the German minister for economic affairs, in a series of comments on the Werner Plan, expressed the hope that its implementation would turn the EEC into a stable community. Mr. Schiller based this hope essentially on the fact that the plan not only provided for coordination of monetary policies but also for more thorough harmonization of financial and economic policy from the outset.

Mr. Schiller clarified his attitude in the December 1970 edition of *Europäische Gemeinschaft*:

I consider the model worked out in the Werner Plan as a good solution and one which is likely to last. This multi-stage plan brings the need for harmonization of economic policy into the center and clearly shows that an economic and monetary union cannot be achieved unilaterally simply by unification of monetary techniques. Only if the common action on monetary policy is based on the solid foundation of a common short-term economic, financial and monetary policy can the Community develop in the long run into a community of stability and growth.[4]

Mr. Emilio Colombo, the Italian minister of finance, was even more categoric that the German officials. On his return to Rome from Paris in February 1970, he told the press that the Common Market would have to adopt a common economic policy before it could hope that a common currency would be created.

Furthermore, the unification of economic policies implies an acceleration of the process of economic integration. It is becoming more and more apparent in these discussions that monetary cooperation aimed at the eventual adoption of a common currency is impossible if economic policies lack not only coordination but unification as well.[5]

At the December 1968 meeting of the Council of Ministers, the EEC Commission Vice-President Barre announced that the Commission would make formal proposals to the Council of Ministers by February 15, 1969 to create a Community mutual aid mechanism in the monetary field. When the European Commission finally submitted its memorandum to the Council on the coordination of economic policies and monetary cooperation within the Community, it was emphasized that the proposals were an organic and indissoluble whole. It was also stressed that they did not concern the monetary field exclusively but made provision at the same time for the coordination of short-term economic policies, coordination of medium-term economic policies, and cooperation with regard to monetary policies. It was clear, therefore, that Mr. Barre and the Commission had been responsive to the split between the member states and had recognized that absolute sovereignty and exclusive responsibility of the governments in the economic area were basically contradictory with the setting up of automatic mutual-aid mechanisms in the monetary area.

The first high-level confrontation on the February 1969 Barre Memorandum took place at the quarterly meeting of the ministers of finance and governors of central banks held in Mons, Belgium, in April. The most critical comments came from the Dutch and the Italians. Mr. Witteveen was particularly concerned that the creation of new monetary mechanisms between the Six would place obstacles in the way of enlarging the Community. Mr. Colombo once again stressed that Italy thought it advisable to establish a close link between the coordination of economic policies and monetary cooperation. This did not necessarily mean, he said, that a consultation mechanism was required for each problem, but that there should be extensive coordination of economic policy aims, at least over the medium term. Mr. François Ortoli, the French minister, was one of the few to come out unequivocally in favor of the plan. The suggestions for monetary cooperation he characterized as "reasonable."[6]

The first discussions of the Barre Memorandum in the Committee of Permanent Representatives revealed a straight split down the middle between the member states—Germany, Italy and Belgium, in support of the draft, against France, Luxembourg and the Netherlands. But even the supporters of the plan expressed differences on the relationship between the coordination of economic policies and monetary cooperation on the one hand and the nature of the monetary support on the other. Belgium claimed that strict discipline in economic coordination would make progress possible in the monetary field. Germany, however, was in favor of parallel economic coordination and monetary cooperation. Italy maintained that there should be compulsory consultations on coordination.

The Permanent Representatives, after three weeks of preparation for the July 17, 1969 Council of Ministers meeting, were able to smooth out some of the differences between the member states, but a considerable number of problems still remained. None of the governments had expressed any doubt about the need to increase coordination in economic and monetary matters. After the monetary problems experienced in the autumn and winter of 1968, each of the member states was well aware that without closer and better structures for coordinating economic policies, they were obliged to take isolated national measures that could jeopardize many of the Community achievements. As a response to short-term economic difficulties, almost all the member states had taken unilateral meaures to protect themselves. Germany had been obliged to introduce export taxes and import tax refunds, France had kept exchange controls, Italy had introduced limitations on capital movements, and the Netherlands had applied price controls.

However, almost all the delegations were extremely cautious about how the measures were to be implemented and exactly what would be the nature and the range of the commitments they were prepared to undertake. A further complication derived from the fact that the Permanent Representatives did not have full responsibility to discuss all aspects of the plan. Some areas came within the province of the central banks or the national budgetary authorities. Others involved mechanisms and procedures that had to be dealt with in international monetary bodies. For this reason the Permanent Representatives asked that the Council meeting should be attended by the chairmen of the different specialized committees: the Committee of Governors of Central Banks, the Monetary Committee, the Budget Policy Committee, the Short-Term Economic Policy Committee, and the Medium-Term Economic Policy Committee.[7]

The decisions adopted at the July 17 meeting of the Council broke ground for the Community. By agreeing in principle to make provision for the joint establishment of medium-term economic policy aims; compulsory consultations on national measures that diverged from these aims or which could have an influence throughout the Community; short-term automatic monetary support in the event of currency difficulties; and medium-term financial assistance, the member states for the first time envisaged measures that would give the Community an overall policy in the economic and monetary areas. But the program was adopted with some reluctance, some reservations and, in some cases, without much enthusiasm on the part of the member states. Mainly, the ministers were persuaded to come to an agreement by their awareness of the increasing interdependence of their economies and their fear that difficulties in one member state would inevitably have repercussions on the others. In his closing comments, Mr. Witteveen, the president of the Council, made it quite clear that the member states had been obliged to opt for lesser evils. Without the coordination of economic policies, the principle of monetary cooperation would not have been accepted by three of the member states. The monetary support mechanism, however, provided an opportunity for financial assistance only if there was agreement on the short-term economic measures.

Although the July 17 decision was greeted with some fanfare, it should not be forgotten that none of the proposed mechanisms was to enter in effect without implementing legislation, and this inevitably made it easier for the ministers to reach their decision. Even the consultations on national measures, the subject of a formal Council decision, were not defined in detail. Finally, the Netherlands was only prepared to agree to the monetary support mechanism on condition that agreement was reached on the means of implementing it. When the Dutch minister was questioned about the significance of this important reservation, Mr. Witteveen stated that the Netherlands would only give its final approval on two conditions: that the Community mechanism fit in with the arrangements for monetary cooperation already in existence outside the Community framework in OECD and the IMF; and that it not weaken measures for economic policy coordination.[8]

It took another six months before the ministers of the Six moved on from expressing hopes about the future of economic and monetary cooperation in the Community to producing some concrete decisions. The incentives for action built up considerably during the second half of 1969. The continued economic and monetary crisis, both inside and outside the Community, and the serious dangers created by increased economic imbalance between the Six pointed up the need for closer cooperation and coordination. In addition, the December 1969 Hague summit conference cleared a great deal of ground for further progress in the weeks after the meeting by producing a kind of "afterglow" effect. Consequently, the ministers were able to reach agreement on the procedures for the prior consultations proposed in July 1969 and on the system of short-term monetary support to be implemented by the Community's central banks.[9]

The Hague summit meeting did much more than provide an incentive for the Council of Ministers to reach some concrete decisions. In January 1970, the Council passed a resolution to establish an economic and monetary union in the Community. In February 1970, the member states presented their own ideas about the ways this union should be brought about. At the quarterly meeting of the ministers of finance held in Paris in the last week of February 1970, three of the ministers, Mr. Schiller of Germany, Baron Snoy et d'Oppuers of Belgium, and Mr. Werner of Luxembourg, submitted fairly detailed plans for establishing the proposed union.

The finance ministers' meeting made it quite clear that the major issue was whether to provide monetary support for member states whose currencies experienced difficulties or whether to integrate the members' economies so that currency problems would not arise. The ministers, unable to reach any compromise decision at the meeting, made their findings and position clear in the final communiqué issued to the press by Mr. Giscard d'Estaing. The six ministers had expressed identical views on two main problems, he said: the need to give Europe some form of monetary organization, in other words, to establish a Community monetary personality; and the financial aims. Opinions did differ, however, on the way the different stages should be established. Consequently, the ministers agreed to recommend the following procedure to the Council of Ministers of the Communities: establishment of a seven-member ad hoc committee composed of the five chairmen of the special committees, Mr. Pierre Werner of Luxembourg, who would chair the committee, and a representative of the EEC Commission. The ad hoc committee would submit proposals to the Council of Ministers within three months on the basis of the various plans that had been presented.

The Werner Committee worked in record time. By the end of May it had already prepared an interim report dealing with the main aspects of the establishment of an economic and monetary union. In an interview with a Luxembourg newspaper, Mr. Werner discussed his committee's progress. He spoke first about the respective authority of the national and European bodies:

As regards the ultimate position towards which we are working, i.e., the final form of the monetary union, I am pleased to point out that a broad measure of agreement was reached in the Committee. The discussion was more lively on the problem of defining, within the framework of the future monetary union, the powers of the European bodies on the one hand and the national bodies on the other. Our discussions led to the realization that even in the final phase of the monetary union, the individual states will still have certain tasks to perform in budgetary and other spheres. Discussions will no doubt continue to center on the problem of defining areas of authority.[10]

Mr. Werner was forced to admit, however, that the old split on priorities —economic union first or monetary union first—had also appeared during his committee's work:

The solution which we propose takes into account the realities. On the one hand we have a proposal to establish a common monetary policy vis-à-vis non-member states in the initial phase. At the same time we feel that real efforts must also be made to coordinate and harmonize economic policies in the initial phase. We are thinking for example of budgetary policy, financial policy and also to some extent of incomes policy. In short we have come to the conclusion that the greatest prospect for success will come from the parallel application of these widely varying measures in particular to the extent that the measures of monetary and economic policy taken with a view to establishing a monetary union will interact favorably.[11]

Despite Mr. Werner's comments, when the report came before the quarterly meeting of finance ministers in Venice at the end of May 1970, the old divisions were still very much alive. Germany, Italy, and the Netherlands continued to insist that integration of national economic policies must precede monetary union, while the EEC Commission, France, Belgium, and Luxembourg urged the simultaneous implementation of integrative measures in both fields. Disagreement had resurfaced over the Werner Report proposal to create a European exchange stabilization fund by the end of the first stage of the economic and monetary union. The German government's opposition to this proposal, as voiced by Mr. Schiller, was unshakable. Germany was afraid that the fund would simply use the Bundesbank reserves to prop up weak EEC currencies, particularly the French franc. The French government, on the other hand, through its spokesman, Mr. Giscard d'Estaing, adopted the most "European" position. Not only did he promote the idea of an exchange stabilization fund, but he also pressed for a reduction in parity margins. Officially, the French justified their stand by putting forward European monetary union as a second and alternative "pole" to the United States and the dollar, a pole they claimed would be vitally necessary to the future of the world monetary system. The division between the member countries was thus far too sharp for any early compromise.[12]

The divergences of the Venice meeting were reiterated at the June 9 meeting of the Council of Ministers. The Werner Report had tried not to refer to the split too directly, but the German and Dutch ministers, in much more forthright terms than had been used in the written report, insisted that the main objective of the first stage must be to coordinate economic policies and that there should be absolutely no question of narrowing the fluctuation of margins between the six currencies or of setting up an exchange stabilization fund during the first stage. The transition to the later stages, according to Mr. Schiller, must be subject to efficient economic policy coordination. Only under those conditions could monetary cooperation assume automatic forms and involve compulsory mechanisms. Mr. Witteveen went even further and raised objections concerning the coordination of the member states' positions in the international monetary organizations, particularly in the IMF. The definition of a joint position, he maintained, should not have a compulsory and restraining nature. The French, Belgian, and Luxembourg approach, on the other hand, was that monetary solidarity would in itself constitute the impetus for the convergence of economic policies. After a lengthy debate, the Council decided to take note of the conclusions of the interim Werner Report and to give the group a mandate to define the contents of the first stage in detail by September 1970.[13]

The final report of the Werner group was eventually completed in the early hours of the morning of October 8, 1970 after seventeen hours of discussion. It was stressed after the marathon meeting that the proposals contained in the report were the "unanimous" findings of the group. In other words, the Werner group had managed to reach a compromise between the German and Dutch "economists" and the French and Belgian "monetarists." However, several factors must be taken into consideration when analyzing this unusually speedy solution. In the first place, the report committed the Six to nothing binding for two years. The first steps would indeed be taken as of 1971, but any treaty rewriting and transfer of sovereignty would not be broached before 1973. Second, although the members of the Werner group worked in close cooperation with the member governments, no real measures could be decided upon before the Council of Ministers of the Communities came out with its findings on the basis of a proposal from the EEC Commission. No sooner had the Werner Report appeared than *Le Monde* was reminding its readers that France was still in a bind. On the one hand, revolt against the hegemony of the dollar necessitated the creation of an alternative "monetary pole" in Europe. On the other hand, *Le Monde* asked, would not a "monetary Europe," like an "industrial Europe," be in danger of domination by the constantly growing German giant?[14]

French objections to some aspects of the Werner Report appear to have been responsible for the changes in the proposal prepared in November by the EEC Commission for submission to the Council of Ministers. Under the heading: "Commission Forwards Werner Proposals—Censored" the weekly *Opera Mundi* commented: "By dint of some nice juggling with form and presentation, the EEC Commission has managed to dispense the ticklish duty of putting the recently published Werner Report on monetary and economic union in the Community into 'acceptable' terms for debate by the EEC Council of Ministers."[15] What the Commission had done was to tone down the more "supranational" elements of the plan. The Commission avoided any mention of the new Community "decision-making center" suggested by the Werner Report. Instead, the Commission said that any transfer of power that took place should go to the existing Community institutions. The Commission also refrained from inviting the member states to make a specific commitment to revise the Rome Treaty by the end of the first three-year phase of the move toward economic and monetary union. The proposed resolution stated that this should be done only if it should prove necessary. Direct mention was also avoided of strengthening the European Parliament. The Commission preferred to talk instead about "democratic control at Community level." These modifications were an attempt to avoid at all costs—for the time being at least—a renewal of the dispute between France and the other member states over supranationality.

When the Commission's proposals first came up for discussion by the Council at the end of November 1970, the member states accorded them high priority. However, there were a number of problems. As Mr. Harmel, the Belgian foreign minister, pointed out afterwards, the Six listened to each other politely, but there was no real dialogue. Press comment on the meeting reflected this general reaction. Philippe Lemaître wrote in *Le Monde*:

It is truly difficult after Monday's exchange of views to obtain an opinion on the intentions of the governments of the Community, on their desire to adopt before the end of the year a program of monetary and economic action going beyond a general declaration of intention on the needs for increased cooperation. Since the ministers were above all prompted by the concern not to commit themselves, not to seek out possible means of compromise at this stage, they repeated what was already perfectly well known.[16]

Pierre Drouin, also writing in *Le Monde*, was much more specific:

The French government, for its part, decided to wait before acting, but no one had any doubts that precisely what the Germans and the Dutch liked most in the Werner Report was a source of great anxiety to the French. They saw in it a new nest of supranational serpents, always ready to hiss above European heads.[17]

Even after almost uninterrupted work by governmental experts and the Committee of Permanent Representatives, when the Council of Ministers met in mid-December there were still broad differences on five fundamental issues: transfer of power, regional and structural policy, powers of the central banks, transition to the later stages, and amendment of the Rome Treaty. After meeting for almost twelve hours, the French position was still no closer to that of the other five governments, and the meeting was adjourned. Various suggestions were made in an attempt to obtain another meeting before the end of the year, including the famous "stopping the clock" procedure, but they were all rejected. Germany's refusal to accept the last suggestion was widely interpreted as a political move, since the German presidency of the Council would be followed by that of France. It was clear that the Germans considered that it was up to those whom they believed to be partially responsible for the lack of agreement to smooth things over in the new year.

Mr. Schiller, in his press conference after the Council meeting, also made it quite clear that he considered the French largely responsible for the ministers' failure. In reply to questions from journalists, he said that the debate had clearly shown that, on the one hand, there was a view of the monetary union, shared by the Commission and most of the member states, which would involve some institutional modifications and, on the other hand, the view of the French delegation, according to which everything must remain within the limits of the Rome Treaty.

There are different views of the union, for us there must be clearly defined competences in order to prevent the Community from becoming a Community of inflation and remain a bloc of stability and growth. We think that the treaty should be amended after the first phase. However, others do not see the relationship between the aims and the institutions.[18]

Attempts to iron out the differences between the member states filled most of January and the first week of February 1971 in preparation for the crucial February 8-9 meeting of the Council of Ministers. In addition to the regular quarterly session of the ministers of finance held in mid-January, there was a whole series of bilateral meeting, most important of all that between French and German representatives. Mr. Colombo of Italy visited Paris and Mr. Barre, vice-president of the EEC Commission also met with a number of the individual ministers.

One of the most important features to emerge from the French-German meeting in January was the German suggestion that a special clause should be introduced into the proposals for the economic and monetary union. The clause provided that in order to ensure parallelism between the monetary and the economic provisions, the first stage for both would last four years. If agreement then failed to be reached on the transition to the second stage, the monetary mechanisms would cease to apply. This "guillotine" clause was intended to avoid one of the most serious stumbling blocks of the negotiations. It made it possible to avoid immediate formal undertakings on moving on to the later stages (thus satisfying France), while at the same time removing the automatic element from the monetary measures if insufficient progress was made in coordinating economic policies (thus allaying German fears).[19]

Agreement on this clause, in slightly modified form, finally broke the logjam and allowed the ministers to reach a decision on February 9 after two days of almost constant debate. The two main antagonists had in fact agreed to bury their differences by postponing a decision on more supranationalism during a trial period of intensified economic and monetary cooperation. The French foreign minister, Maurice Schumann, president of the Council, told the press that this technique avoided "false steps" and showed "a political will married to the pragmatic approach." The Dutch secretary of state for foreign affairs, Mr. A.J. de Koster, also put the compromise in the form of an analogy: "We are like the couple who have an engagement party. If over the next five years we don't get married, we return the gifts."[20] The six member states had taken themselves off the hook by reaching an agreement that was both tentative and reversible. The really hard commitments had been postponed for three years.

The postponement of final, binding decisions seems to be the clue to many of the compromises that were made. In point of fact, although there was a reasonable amount of give-and-take on the desirability and broad aims of the union, when the chips were down, the "economists" were not much closer to the "monetarists" than they had been two years earlier, nor were the French more inclined than they had been earlier to talk in concrete terms of supranational institutions and central decision-making authorities. As one official close to the Communities commented: "You must distinguish between decisions that are decisions and decisions that are not really decisions."[21] Elaborating on this, he suggested that the only decisions worthy of the name were those that stood a good chance of being implemented within a reasonable period of time. In the first place, the February 9, 1971 decision on the economic and monetary union left much that was vague. Second, all the member states were well aware that the very fragile structure begun in 1971 could be toppled by events on the international monetary scene. Even though the member states may have wanted to establish an ambitious and innovatory union throughout the two years of negotiation, they fell back to the known, secure, well-constructed lines of national concerns.

The first image is, therefore, one of governmental representatives who stood by their national positions until the very last moment. Only when they were able to work out a formula that left the substantive issues so vague or so flexible as to be almost meaningless were they able to reach agreement. If we turn from the governments to the grass-roots and the representative groups, we see a much clearer picture, one in which the interest groups were able to convince the man in the street that his material well-being would best be served by economic and monetary union.

Image II: The Myth of the Sensitized Public

The economic and monetary union proposals encountered little opposition from interest groups in the Community and from the national parliaments, since all concerned recognized that the six member economies had grown increasingly interdependent, that disturbances in one country inevitably had harmful effects in the others, and that many sectors of the economy had much to gain by greater economic and monetary cooperation and, ultimately, union. Mr. Barre, one of the prime movers of the economic and monetary union, made the situation very clear in a speech before the Fifth International Investment Symposium in June 1970:

The monetary disturbances which afflicted the Community in 1969 and the serious difficulties the international monetary system ran into have made the public more and more sensitive to the internal and international monetary aspects of our Community venture: only the specialist can really grasp how elaborate and sophisticated machinery works, but the public has realized how important it is in practice and in politics. I think we should be unwise to disappoint the man in the street on this important issue.[22]

In fact, even though EEC officials stressed the public's interest in economic and monetary union, pressure was exerted by trade and industrial groups at all levels. As one official from the Union nationale des industries du marché commun (UNICE) pointed out: "It is important for us in industry to give constant backing to the development of an economic union and, in order to achieve this, we must exert a moral influence on the EEC Commission and on the member governments."[23] In line with this philosophy, in December 1970, UNICE issued a position paper broadly supportive of the Werner Report and the EEC Commission proposals:

UNICE is in favor of a Community policy for establishing economic and monetary union, which will be a major step in European integration. By moving towards economic and monetary union, the governments will be giving evidence of the political will they demonstrated at The Hague.[24]

The Association of EEC Savings Banks also played an active part in supporting the Community institutions by circulating opinions among the press and national officials at regular intervals. In September 1970, the Association adopted a highly positive recommendation on the economic and monetary union plans. The achievement of a European monetary union, the Association stated, would depend on the will of the peoples and governments to cede important sovereign rights concerning internal and external monetary policy, short-term economic policy, and tax policy to supranational bodies.[25]

Just one week before the Council of Ministers' final decision on February 9, 1971, the Association issued another position paper on the introduction of a multistage plan for economic and monetary union. Still very much in favor of the union, the Association was critical of both the Werner group and the EEC Commission for watering down their proposals. The Association stated that the "political significance" and "irreversible nature" ascribed to the union and the introduction of "democratic control" at Community level required a clear and formal resolve by the member states, before the beginning of the first stage, to accept a political union. The Association was also critical of some of the economic policy proposals. It maintained that it was absolutely essential to safeguard monetary stability in future decisions on the economic and monetary union.[26]

Community trade organizations also made an early start on publicizing those aspects of the proposals that met with their support. In September 1969, the Council of European Trade Federations and the Committee of Commercial Organizations of the EEC held a meeting in Amsterdam to study in detail the question of European economic and monetary policy. The gap between the two, it claimed, had led to many serious disturbances in intra-Community trade. The two trade organizations thus asked the member states

that their policy, at national levels as well as within the framework of the Council of

Ministers, should take better account of the needs of the Common Market. Instead of breaking the natural expansion of the EEC economy by an incoherent policy, because it is in the first place inspired by national interests, the governments should set up—as the Treaty of Rome lays down—before the end of the transition period, and based on the national economies of the member countries, an authentic and dynamic community, pursuing a common, obligatory policy in the economic, market and monetary spheres, as well as in the sphere of external economic relations.[27]

National groups representing trade and industry also actively pressured their governments to support the proposed economic and monetary union. At a July 1970 session of the French Economic and Social Council, Mr. André Malterre, chairman of the Confédération générale des cadres (executive personnel), stated:

We must ask ourselves whether it would not be desirable to make more rapid progress towards a European monetary union in order to build up a bipolar monetary system in which the European currency would be able to counterbalance the dollar. To achieve this aim it is of course essential to reject any system based on fluctuating exchange rates in the European Economic Community. We must also work towards harmonization of business cycle policy in the different Common Market countries.[28]

On the eve of the Council of Ministers' marathon in February 1971, the German Chambers of Industry and Commerce warned against any "weakening" of the Werner Plan as a result of compromises and package deals. In a letter to the Federal minister for economic and financial affairs, Karl Schiller, Mr. Paul Broicher, the chairman of the Chambers, wrote that agreement on the basic features of the desired economic and monetary union had to be reached before any final decisions or measures were taken in the monetary field. The Chambers went on to assert that, in a European economic and monetary union, economic, cyclical, and monetary policies would have to be laid down by central Community institutions. The Community decision-making body for this could not be the Council of Ministers, where the individual member states had the right of veto. On the contrary, the institutions must be able to lay down a unified European economic, cyclical, and monetary policy independently of any national directions, and for this purpose, national powers would have to be transferred to a new executive body.[29] This highly influential German pressure group was, therefore, pressing a policy almost identical to that adopted by Mr. Schiller throughout the negotiation of the economic and monetary union proposals.

In influential Italian trade circles there was also considerable similarity between the views advanced by the representative groups and the line defended by Italian government spokesmen in Community ministerial meetings. At the end of November 1970, the Italian branch of the International Chamber of Commerce met in Rome to discuss various aspects of the international monetary system and in particular the Werner Plan. After outlining the various stages laid down in the plan, Dr. Rinaldo Ossola, economic adviser to the Bank of Italy, said that there was a tendency to emphasize the monetary aspect. The Werner Plan, he said, laid down clear objectives, but the aims had been blurred in the EEC Commission's proposals. At the same meeting, Dr. Frances Mattei, one of Italy's leading industrialists, said that technical objections could be made to the Werner Plan, but the political proposals could not be rejected. The time had come to move from economic union to a supranational union, he declared.[30]

While economic groups in the member states were making their opinions on the proposed economic and monetary union known to their governments and to the public, the Community's own body representing industry, labor and services—the Economic and Social Committee—also regularly submitted its views to the EEC Commission. Like the national groups, the Economic and Social Committee came out from the beginning very much in favor of the proposed union. In its first report on the subject, drawn up by Mr. Louis Ameye for the specialized section on economic questions and presented in September 1969, the specialized section maintained that the achievement of monetary aims was always in danger of being jeopardized so long as there were divergences in the economic policies of the member states. Any prolonged divergence would inevitably end up in severe monetary problems. Moreover, the report went on, the monetary mechanisms proposed in the Barre Plan would become meaningless, since mutual competition would be likely to promote divergent economic policies.[31]

The need to coordinate economic policies within the framework of the proposed economic and monetary union was reiterated at intervals by the Economic and Social Committee right up to the passage of the February 1971 decision. The Committee was quite prepared to admit that the monetary aspects of the union were very important, but, it asserted, over the long term and even over the medium term, the success of a monetary policy was largely based on the existence of a coordinated economic policy and, above all, on the political will of the member states to achieve this coordination. In the achievement of a coordinated economic policy, the Committee said, the contribution of the economic and social sectors would be considerable, in particular that of the Economic and Social Committee, which had always supported such policy coordination. It hoped that it would be able to make an active contribution to all the phases of the achievement of the economic and monetary union.[32]

Although the Economic and Social Committee served only in an advisory capacity on the economic and monetary union proposals, as one of the Committee's officials explained, it played quite a crucial relaying role. The EEC Commission has almost no direct access to reactions in the member states. The groups representing economic and social interests on the national level, for example, have very little access to the Commission during the initial stages of the preparation of texts, whereas the Economic and Social Committee does. Admittedly, the Community federations of economic and social organizations lobby the Commission on a regular basis, but the federations have to contend with a great deal of independent action on the part of their member national associations. More often than not, the national bodies do not follow the guidelines set out by the Brussels central federation. Rather, the reverse tends to be true, and the Brussels offices try to be responsive to the diverse reactions emerging from the six national capitals.

Officials of the Economic and Social Committee stressed time and again that membership in the Committee and its specialized sections had a strong socializing, "Europeanizing" effect on the counselors. As one official pointed out: "It is important for the counselors to hear the views of members of other nationalities in the debates. They must learn to understand the others. It is the socializing of the counselors themselves that is more important than the actual opinions issued by the Committee. When they return to their own countries, they see things in a different light."[33] More than one official pointed out that the members of the Economic and Social Committee felt considerably freer to adopt an independent approach within the Committee than they were able to do in their own countries, and that it was the one Community body where the Commission and the Council were able to get away from opinions evolved on the basis of the lowest common denominator.

One exception to the general support for the broad aims of the economic and monetary union came from labor circles. The unions were concerned over the lack of social policy provisions in the economic and monetary union proposals. This was the central theme of the statement issued in May 1970 by the European Confederation of Free Trade Unions in the Community. After examining the EEC Commission's proposals, the Confederation's executive committee stated:

Once again an important proposal by the Commission makes no provision for concrete action in the social sector. Consequently, [the executive committee] demands that the plan should be completed by Community measures with regard to employment, working conditions and social security. At the same time, in the action envisaged by the plan, the Community cannot limit itself to a simple mission of harmonization but it must see to it that social justice is achieved.

In order to protect labor interests, a tripartite committee (EEC Commission and member governments/employers/labor) was asked for which would issue opinions on the various measures taken to institute the economic and monetary union. The unions called for discussions at least twice a year on the relations between general economic and monetary and social policy.[34]

On the left wing of the labor movement, adverse reactions to the economic and monetary union were even stronger. In April 1970 the EEC Commission received a delegation from the Standing Committee of the Italian and French left-wing unions (CGIL-CGT). An economic and monetary union would help certain large multinational companies or groups to extend their economic and financial domination, which, the delegation maintained, had always had very adverse social consequences.[35] A few months later, in January 1971, the Italian General Confederation of Labor made its opposition to the Werner Plan and the EEC Commission's proposals very clear:

The Werner Plan in fact gives a predominant role to monetary maneuvers and through stringent machinery for coordination at Community level it completely ties the hands of national economic policy. It will help to isolate still further economic policy options from closer contact with trade union and democratic pressures at the very time when decisive powers are being entrusted to the central banks. . . . Once again the option proposed in the Werner Plan lessens the value of any effective political undertaking . . . and it confirms the notion that social and employment policy are minor matters which are apparently to be totally subordinate to economic choices.[36]

The unions found themselves in a rather awkward position. Basically, they were hard put to challenge the entire concept of the economic and monetary union, since it was recognized by all except the left-wing groups as a positive step on the road toward European integration. On the other hand, there was no denying that the proposals put forward by the EEC Commission and the Werner group were likely to strengthen big business. It is hardly surprising that one ranking labor union official, when questioned about the economic and monetary union proposals, responded with a contemptuous gesture. "The economic union decision," he said, "is an excellent example of a nondecision. The preparation of decisions of that amplitude takes years. Deciding on the details of a complete economic and monetary union in just over a year is plainly impossible."[37]

The belief that the creation of an economic and monetary union between the member countries of the European Community was a rather utopian idea was not restricted to the labor unions. It also occupied a fairly large place in the press, which particularly criticized the political aspects of the proposed union. Newspapers in France, Germany, and the Netherlands all asked whether the member countries were prepared to pay the political price of the operation.[38] In other words, the press was in a similar position to that of the representative groups: although they might disagree with the different methods proposed, to attack the principles of the economic and monetary union plan risked branding themselves as anti-

European. Only the extreme left wing dared do this. Consequently, even where there was considerable dissatisfaction with the proposed union, its opponents had to content themselves with chipping away at details. Moreover, the details were frequently so technical that the press and the interest groups were only able to touch on them. It was all very well for Vice-President Barre to declare that the ordinary people of the member countries felt the disturbing effects of inflation, monetary problems on the international scene, and devaluations and revaluations of currencies. In reality, there was very little scope for expression of protest or support when it came to discussing the width of parity bands, margins of fluctuation, and establishing reserve funds. Unlike the discontented farmers, who could take to the streets and protest the prices of their products, there was really very little that "the public" could do when presented with vague, incomprehensible projects for measures to be implemented a decade later.

It seems, therefore, that the decision to introduce an economic and monetary union in the European Community was not substantially influenced by grass-roots and interest group pressures. Trade, big business, and industry clearly had much to gain by the elimination of economic and monetary barriers between the EEC member countries. Consequently, it was easy for them to come out almost unreservedly in favor of the Community's proposals and to encourage the institutions to move forward. But labor union requests for the intermeshing of social policy with economic and monetary policy went almost unheeded. Left-wing protests that big business would run rampant were ignored. Apparently the public was well aware that inflation and recession are acutely uncomfortable conditions. This was nothing new, and there are no significant signs that they associated it with long-term corrective proposals submitted by far-off institutions. As far as can be judged from this second look at the economic and monetary union decision, only a very small additional dimension is gained by looking at it through a nongovernmental lens.

Image III: Overlapping Functions

By very reason of its technicality, economic and financial policy on both the national and international levels falls automatically within the domain of a small, highly trained, highly qualified group of experts in each country. It was pointed out that from the end of World War II, with the establishment of the different international monetary organizations subsequent to the Bretton Woods agreement, financial and economic experts and government officials came together regularly at meetings of the International Monetary Fund, the World Bank, the various specialized agencies of the United Nations, OECD, and the Basel Club of the Group of Ten. As a result, when the European Economic Community was set up in 1958, many of the economic and monetary experts and government officials in the six member states already knew each other well. Events on the international and European monetary scene during the 1960s forced the EEC authorities to develop even closer and more effective coordination in the area. In its ninth annual report, the Monetary Committee of the European Community pointed out that two years earlier, in 1965, it had already discussed the implications of the trend toward de facto monetary integration. It had stated then that the completion of the common agricultural policy and the customs union would intensify capital movements between the member states. "In these circumstances," the report stated, "advances in the coordination of economic and monetary policies are proving necessary. . . . Co-ordination work must increasingly assume the form of consultations prior to every economic or monetary decision which will affect in any appreciable degree the economic development of other Member States."[39]

This coordination process had been strengthened and extended by the establishment of a number of specialized Community institutions: the Short-Term Economic Policy Committee in 1960 and, in 1964, the Budget Policy Committee, the Committee of Governors of Central Banks, and the Medium-Term Economic Policy Committee. The ministers of finance of the six member states also met regularly four times a year in a semiofficial capacity. In other words, the European Community had provided itself, over a period of four or five years, with an elaborate structure of specialized, highly technical committees and groups that inevitably involved a certain amount of overlapping membership.

As an illustration of the overlapping membership of the different specialized committees, it is illuminating to examine the membership and official functions of the Monetary Committee in 1969-70. Until the end of September 1969, the Committee was chaired by Mr. E. van Lennep, treasurer general in the Netherlands ministry of finance. Mr. van Lennep left the Monetary Committee when he was appointed secretary general of OECD. Mr. van Lennep was replaced by one of the two vice-chairmen, Mr. Clappier, deputy governor of the Banque de France, who was in his turn replaced by Professor Drees, treasurer general in the Netherlands ministry of finance. The second vice-chairman of the Committee was Dr. Otto Emminger, a vice-president of the Deutsche Bundesbank. The other members of the Committee included the director general for economic and financial affairs and the director for monetary affairs of the EEC Commission staffs; from banking circles, a director of the Banque Nationale de Belgique, a director of the Nederlandsche Bank, a deputy director of the Banca d'Italia, and a member of the board of the Luxembourg Caisse d'Epargne de l'Etat. On the governmental experts' side, the Committee included: a director general from the Belgian ministry of finance, a director from the Federal Republic's ministry of economic affairs, a director from the French ministry of economic and financial affairs, a governmental adviser from the Luxembourg treasury department and the head of the Italian general accounting office.[40]

An even more telling example of overlapping functions is the composition of the famous Werner group, an ad hoc committee, set up in accordance with the Council decision of March 6, 1970 to draw up a report on the phased establishment of an economic and monetary union in the European Community. The group took its name from its chairman, Mr. Pierre Werner, Luxembourg prime minister and minister of finance. The group had six members in addition to Mr. Werner: Mr. Clappier, chairman of the Monetary Committee; Mr. Stammati, chairman of the Budget Policy Committee (also a member of the Monetary Committee); Professor Brouwers, chairman of the Short-Term Economic Policy Committee; Mr. Schöllhorn, chairman of the Medium-Term Economic Policy Committee (also a secretary of state in the German ministry of economic affairs); Baron Ansiaux, chairman of the Committee of Governors of the Central Banks; and Mr. Ugo Mosca, director general of the EEC Commission's directorate general for economic and financial affairs (also a member of the Monetary Committee). The secretary of the Werner group was Mr. Morelli, secretary of the Monetary Committee.[41] It is hardly surprising, therefore, to learn that at the annual meeting of the International Monetary Fund in Copenhagen in 1970, so many members of the Werner group were present in their national capacities that they were able to put the finishing touches to their proposals to the EEC Council of Ministers for bringing into being the proposed economic and monetary union in the Community.[42]

It has already been noted in connection with the Monetary Committee and the Werner group that both included upper-level officials from the EEC Commission's directorate general for economic and financial affairs. In addition, many of the high-ranking personnel from this directorate general (D.G. II) came from circles in the national administration very similar to those from which the members of the various experts' committees were drawn. Frequently, their educational and professional backgrounds closely resembled those of the economic and monetary policy advisers to the permanent representations of the member states in Brussels, much more so than in other policy areas. Officials from D.G. II provided the secretariats for all the specialized committees with the exception of that of the Committee of Governors of Central Banks, which guarded its autonomy with considerable jealousy. It is hardly surprising, therefore, that a close "old school tie" network existed, particularly between the EEC Commission staff and the staffs of the Permanent Representatives.

Another unusual feature of policy-making in the area of economic and financial affairs was the quarterly meetings of the ministers of finance of the member countries. These meetings were not officially meetings of the Council of Ministers. In fact, their status was rather ambiguous. Written questions to both the Council of Ministers and to the EEC Commission were put on four occasions in 1969 and three occasions in 1970 asking whether or not the meetings of the finance ministers should be considered as meetings of the Council and if not, why not. On each occasion, the Council or the Commission replied that the meetings had no formal status as Council sessions. Nevertheless, the meetings provided some of the most important interchanges and political debates of the economic and monetary union negotiations. Unlike the meetings of the Council of Ministers, which were almost always held in Luxembourg or Brussels, the quarterly meetings of the finance ministers rotated between the different member countries. Nor were they necessarily held in a capital city. Moreover, instead of the meeting being chaired by the representative of the country chairing the Community for that six-month period, the meetings of the finance ministers were chaired by the chief representative of the host country. Thus, the April 1969 meeting was held in Mons, Belgium and was chaired by Baron Snoy et d'Oppuers, and the June 1970 meeting was held in Venice and was chaired by Mr. Emilio Colombo.

To complete the already well-established network of encounters in many different contexts, these meetings of the finance ministers were usually attended by the governors of the Central Banks; the vice-president of the EEC Commission in charge of economic and monetary affairs, Raymond Barre; other members of the EEC Commission; the chairmen of the various specialized committees; and, from outside the immediate Community framework, the chairman of the alternate members of the Group of Ten (OECD), Mr. Rinaldo Ossola (also, incidentally, a member of the Monetary Committee of the Community). These meetings of the finance ministers provided a slightly more relaxed framework for discussion where the ministers could feel under fewer contraints than under the spotlight of the official Council of Ministers sessions.

With such frequent encounters among government officials, Commission staff, and experts, it was hardly surprising that certain individuals came to play a prominent part in a number of the groups. This was particularly true of the Werner Committee. One startling feature of the committee's work was the speed with which it accomplished its task. It drew up an interim report in three months and produced its final report only just over six months after it started deliberating. (Nor should it be forgotten that the summer vacation period occurred in the midst of this.) One of the reasons for this rapidity, one EEC Commission official explained, was that the group met once every ten-to-fourteen days and, although provision was made for replacement members, there were in fact remarkably few absences from the meetings. As a result, there soon emerged what the same official called a real "esprit de corps."

The "esprit de corps" was, however, not only the result of regular meetings. It drew its life to a large degree from the personalities of the members of the committee and, above all, its chairman. Pierre Werner played a role described by one official close to the group as a "good father of the family. He was extremely easy to get along with and we needed him in that group to smooth out problems and keep things on an even keel."[43] Things had to be kept "on an even keel" because the group had its share of strong personalities. Baron Ansiaux of Belgium had a very strong impact on the group, and he was its only member who represented the banking community. He was, however, known to be on extremely good terms with the Belgian minister of finance, Baron Snoy et d'Oppuers. Mr. Clappier of France constituted to some extent the motor force of the group. But he was quite often rivaled by Mr. Schöllhorn of Germany, an extremely dynamic individual, known for his occasional angry outbursts.

In fact, Mr. Schöllhorn, as secretary of state for economic affairs, provided the only visible link with the member governments. The actual links between the members of the Werner group and their respective governments are extremely difficult to trace. Even some of the officials closest to the group admitted to being rather mystified by the precise nature of the coordination between the national authorities and the group members. As one official pointed out: "We had our surprises and the big surprises came from France." Apparently the line adopted by Mr. Clappier in the group was consistent with the French governmental view for some time. Then, without warning, Paris changed direction and went back on the agreement that had been reached with the Germans on the question of supranationalism.

The Germans, not only in the framework of the Werner group, but across the board, had been afraid of the other countries pulling them into economic instability. There had been a considerable amount of bargaining and political give-and-take, and the Germans had been prepared to make some sacrifices. On the French side, things had been going well and everyone believed that agreement was more or less assured. Then, all of a sudden the change came "from the Elysée." As one official pointed out, the reasons for the French change were not too clear, since "Clappier had taken his precautions in the monetary field and Schöllhorn had accepted, but even on the monetary question the French changed their attitude." Possibly, another official suggested, the push came from the extreme Gaullist wing in France. Another reason put forward for the French change was the influence of the British application for membership in the Community. The French may have wanted to make things more difficult for the British, or on the other hand, the Dutch, Germans and Italians may have been trying to negotiate in line with British wishes. The overall result was a sharp clash between the French and the Germans, the removal by the EEC Commission from its proposals of mention of a central decision-making body, a deadlocked Council of Ministers meeting in December 1970, and final agreement in February 1971 only on the basis of the German "guillotine" clause.[44]

As far as individuals were concerned, the economic and monetary union case provides an interesting contrast with the agricultural case. In the agricultural case there was one charismatic personality in the Commission, Mr. Mansholt, working with a group of relatively unknown colleagues both in the national governments and on the Commission staff. In the Werner group, among the ministers, and even among the ranking D.G. II officials in the EEC Commission, a number of men had reputations as individualists. In the Werner group Baron Ansiaux and Mr. Werner himself, whom Commissioner Barre singled out in a speech before the European Parliament because "at a time when economic and monetary union was not fashionable and lacked champions as enthusiastic and zealous as those who have come to the fore in the last few months [he] had always supported the Commission's efforts."[45] Among the ministers, Mr. Schiller and Mr. Giscard d'Estaing played a highly individual role in their country's politics and in European Community affairs.

In the midst of all these individualists, the vice-president of the Commission, Raymond Barre, played a role that is extremely difficult to categorize. He, like his fellow vice-president, Sicco Mansholt, had his two plans named for him, yet his name never seems to have evoked the same kind of love-hate response among his colleagues, aides, associates, and the public at large as that of his colleague. Nonetheless, Mr. Barre was not a personality to be treated lightly. Ray Vicker, writing in *The Wall Street Journal* shortly after the February 1971 decision to create an economic and monetary union in the Community, described him:

Currently, 85 Common Market officials . . . are charting ways to implement economic and monetary union over the next decade. They're working under the diplomatic but tenacious Prof. Barre. This Western-movie fan who says John Wayne is his hero has won a goodly number of fights in the Common Market and is a dogged lobbyist for European unity.[46]

Although Commissioner Barre, an academic by background, tended to avoid the kind of public appearance that Mr. Mansholt appeared to thrive on, he was nonetheless present and active in all the diverse groups, committees, councils, and meetings dealing with the proposed economic and monetary union. In addition to his ubiquity at meetings, Mr. Barre, without great fanfare, also did his share of visiting the various ministries in the member capitals for bilateral talks with the responsible officials in efforts to smooth over difficulties and engineer compromises. He was particularly active in this area during the month and a half between the deadlocked December 1970 Council of Ministers' meeting and the February 8-9, 1971 meeting at which the final compromise decision was reached.

After following the steps leading up to the February 9, 1971 decision to establish an economic and monetary union in stages over a ten-year period from three different perspectives, the weight of evidence tends to bear out the thesis that, in this particular case, the bulk of the decision-making was carried out by the national authorities within the framework of the Council of Ministers. The decision was reached after lengthy, at times frustrating, at times acrimonious debate on methods not principles. At times it seemed there could be no common meeting ground between the national priorities. The sharp discrepancy in philosophy between the two "big powers" of the Community, France and Germany, only served to aggravate the clash of national concerns.

Bearing these differences in mind, it is surprising that a decision was reached with such rapidity, particularly in an area that had always been a jealously guarded national preserve. Perhaps one explanation for the rapidity of the decision was the belief held in many quarters in the Community that political union depended in part on the success of achieving an economic and monetary union. Also, the members were acutely aware that, because of economic and monetary developments taking place both outside and inside the EEC, it was no longer possible for any one country to look exclusively to its own interests.

The second analysis provides us with another possible explanation for the unusual rapidity. In none of the other four case studies discussed were the representative groups in the Community so strongly behind EEC policy. Like the national governments, they may not have been very strongly behind the various methods suggested for instituting the union, but, with one exception only, they were behind the concept of the union as a means toward greater European integration. Thus, the initiators of the plans in the Commission were able to press ahead in the knowledge that the member governments would receive little opposition from their electorates and their influential industrial and labor constituencies.

The third image presented some interesting new aspects of economic and monetary decision-making processes. It shed some light on the emergence in the EEC of what may be described as an international economic and financial elite. This was a community of experts and technocrats, most of whom knew each other well, many of whom had been trained at the same schools, worked at very similar jobs (either in their national capitals or in EEC headquarters in Brussels), attended the same meetings all over the world—in short, a small, exclusive community of experts within a larger community, the European Economic Community.

As Robert Russell, in his study of small group behavior in international monetary negotiations, suggests: "The institutions merely provided supporting services for a travelling circus containing nearly the same performers, and quite often virtually the same performances repeated again and again on demand."[47]

In conclusion, therefore, it is suggested that in the case of economic and monetary decision-making, intergovernmental political processes overlap considerably with small-group, elite network processes. According to the first image, although the national representatives came to know each other well through lengthy and arduous negotiations and repeated conferences, this knowledge had little significant impact on the outcome of the negotiations. The third image, on the other hand, brought to light the "potential for the group process itself to lead to outcomes for national policies which are not a simple combination of aims, resources, and actions of abstract national actors."[48] Patterns of interaction became individualized, and efforts were made to convince other individuals to join in the group consensus, rather than negotiating among the nations toward a mutually acceptable agreement. It is suggested that this was the prime reason why the European Community was able to reach a decision so quickly on measures that would bring about the most fundamental change in the relationships between the member states in the Community's history.

8

Conclusion: A Link Between the Models?

At the beginning of this study, it was suggested that one of the major shortcomings of much of the research conducted into decision-making processes in the European Community has been its single-minded approach. There has been a constant, determined search for a single explanation of the decision-making process. If the researcher could only be diligent enough, if the maze could only be followed carefully enough in all its intricacies and mapped out in sufficient detail, at some point the real center of decision-making could be found, and the individuals, groups, and institutions exerting the real influence could be located.

These efforts had a certain validity in the early years of the European Community's existence. Until 1962 or 1963, the still-growing institutional structure of the Community and the first tasks that it set itself had not become so complex as to suggest that decision-making could, in fact, be many different processes at once. It is also possible to argue that the Community, in its first years, was carried forward by the momentum of the "integrationists" of the 1940s and 1950s, who believed that a truly supranational governing body was a prerequisite for a united Europe. The Community institutions were staffed then by many of the old-line fighters for the cause of European unity. A very convincing argument was put forward by Leon Lindberg in his 1963 study; *The Political Dynamics of European Economic Integration,* that a real center of decision-making was indeed being formed in the EEC Commission in the first years of the European Community's existence.[1]

The Lindberg analysis, however convincing it may be, was published in 1963 and based on research carried out even earlier. Also, the study focuses almost exclusively on a single area of Community activity, agricultural policy-making. Here again, the findings are convincing, but for that particular area of Community activity alone. Lindberg did not address himself at that time to determining whether his conclusions necessarily held good for areas of European Community activity other than agriculture. It was not until his 1970 study, written in collaboration with Stuart Scheingold, *Europe's Would-Be Polity*, that Lindberg dealt with other areas of Community activity (transport policy, the coal sector, the general customs union) and came to the conclusion that the earlier findings no longer applied, or applied in part only.[2]

The 1965-66 "crisis" in the Community brought about a change of attitude among observers, and a new type of decision-making analysis became popular. The new generation of analysts concluded that, when the chips of national interest were finally down, it was the governments of the six member states, not the EEC Commission, who made the crucial decisions. They saw the French walk-out from Community activity in July 1965 and the subsequent humbling of the EEC Commission in the January 1966 Luxembourg settlement as the start of a new trend in Community decision-making or as the reemergence of an old trend that had been obscured until then by the novel role initially played by the EEC Commission. After 1966, analysts began to play down the role of the EEC Commission and to underscore the importance of national pressures exerted in the Council of Ministers and in the Committee of Permanent Representatives. Gordon Adam's study of the European Community's relationships with its African associates is an outstanding example of this type of analysis.[3]

In the opening chapter of this study it was indicated that while many analysts have singled out for detailed examination a specific area of activity, or a particular institution or group, and others have adopted a more general, overall approach, all have attempted to find a single center of decision-making. It was hypothesized that neither of these approaches was fully adequate, for neither made adequate provision for the possibility that there were numerous decision-making processes in the Community and that the salient features of the processes depended on many different variables. The subject being dealt with, the time at which it was being considered, the men, groups and institutions involved, and external pressures were cited as examples of such variables.

In order to verify this hypothesis, add some richness to the earlier analyses, and obtain greater insight into European Community decision-making processes, a methodology was borrowed from foreign policy analysis and adapted to the special conditions obtaining in the European Community. The methodology consisted of selecting three different approaches to decision-making analysis (conceptual schemes) and five cases of decision-making for intensive study. Each of the five case studies was analyzed through the lens of each of the three conceptual schemes in turn. By doing this in every instance, it became apparent that an attempt to understand the decision as a one-model decision only left us with an incomplete explanation of the processes at work. In every instance, changing the conceptual lens through which the case was viewed added new features and new richness. After doing this successively for all five case studies, a whole range of hitherto neglected (or possibly newly emerged) characteristics was brought to light.

For the purposes of analysis, it would perhaps be useful first to examine the ways in which some of the earlier findings were modified by the present study. It has already been mentioned that during the early years of the

European Community's existence, it was widely maintained that the EEC Commission held the reins of power. Then, after the 1965-66 "crisis," these reins were taken over by the member governments. Thus, the Community, after moving toward a supranational type of structure for a few years, veered around and became a kind of mutant intergovernmental organization.

In two of the five case studies (agricultural structures and generalized tariff preferences), the three-lens analysis indicated that, in a general way, the main impetus for the initiation, preparation, and passage of the final decisions did indeed appear to come from the EEC Commission. However, as far as the decision on agricultural structures and prices was concerned, the analysis made it amply clear that it was initiated, prepared, and approved under very special conditions. In the first place, it was not so much the EEC Commission as a whole that provided the impetus for the decision but a single member of the Commission, Sicco Mansholt, and his personal staff who were largely responsible for the entire configuration of the structural reform policy. But even with this example of vigorous Commission initiative, rivalries between the French who wished to obtain as many advantages as they could for their agriculture, and the Germans, who objected to paying the price of reforming French agriculture for the sake of European unity, forced Mr. Mansholt and the EEC Commission to modify extensively their agricultural reform plans. Some light was also thrown on the crucial role played in the few months prior to the final decision by the national and European farmers' organizations (particularly the COPA) in redirecting the Commission's policy suggestions. It was as a result of their pressure that the structural aspect of the proposals was deemphasized in favor of attaching greater importance to price measures.

The decision to introduce tariff preferences to all overseas developing countries was also a Commission-sponsored decision with a number of highly individual characteristics. The subject was under consideration not only in the EEC but also in a number of international organizations, particularly UNCTAD and OECD. The EEC Commission participated in meetings of these international organizations as an observer only. Therefore, one could have expected decisions on the subject to be taken by the member states of the Community. The first analysis indicated that there were indeed wide divergences and, at times, sharp clashes among the member states on the means of introducing the aid to the developing countries. There were disputes too over the rights and privileges already accorded the eighteen African associates of the Community. France strongly supported special privileges for the African associates, since the majority of them were former French dependencies with which France still maintained highly beneficial commercial ties. The Dutch, on the other hand, were quite prepared to sacrifice the African associates, since they had always harbored a certain resentment over what they regarded as paying off the French during the negotiation of Part IV of the Rome Treaty and the Yaoundé conventions. Only after further examination did it become apparent that the driving force behind the entire scheme was located in the EEC Commission. However, just as in the agricultural structures case, it did not come from the Commission as a whole, nor even from one particular directorate general of the Commission, but from one small group inside the external relations directorate general.

Thus, even where it is reasonably established that the main decision-making impetus came from the EEC Commission, the finding has to be qualified. In one case the drive came from the charismatic personality of a single man; in the second case, the drive came from the persistance, skillful public relations efforts, and, at times, near presumptuousness of a small group of high-level European Commission officials. This particular small group worked together over a long period of time, developed a strong group spirit, and carved out for itself a special little fiefdom that it jealously guarded against the encroachments of other groups in the bureaucracy, so that its members became known both within the Community and in a number of international organizations as the EEC's "preferentialists."

Turning to the contention of some analysts that the member governments are the real source of power in the European Community and that, in the final analysis, it is their interests that carry the day, two of the case studies would have borne this out if a three-lens analysis had not been carried out. Both the negotiation of the association agreements with Morocco and Tunisia and the decision to introduce an economic and monetary union in the Community by 1980 appeared to be examples of intergovernmental decision-making.

For the EEC Commission to negotiate the Maghreb association agreements, a mandate from the Council of Ministers was needed. Because of conflicting interests between the French, the Italians, and the Dutch, the Council initially gave the Commission only a very partial negotiating mandate. Then the "crisis" in the Community intervened in 1965, and all external relations negotiations were practically paralyzed. By the time the member states were able to smooth out their differences and give the EEC Commission a new mandate to draft association treaties, the negotiations had been dragging on for so long that the Maghreb countries were prepared to accept very little.

This is the picture of decision-making that emerges when a detailed examination is made through the intergovernmental politics lens alone. By changing lenses, new images became visible. First, a whole set of pressures emerged from pro-Jewish, anti-Arab public opinion in the Netherlands, channeled through to the Council via the Dutch members of the European Parliament. Second, different explanations were obtained for Italy's consistent obstruction in the Council of Ministers to the negotiation of separate agreements with the three Maghreb countries. After examining pressure group activity, it became clear that much of Italy's agricultural production, particularly in the south and in Sicily, would have encountered severe competition from the Maghreb countries if preferential trade conditions had been granted Morocco and Tunisia. There were strong fears that Italian agriculture would be unable to withstand North African competition, since labor in the Maghreb countries was cheaper than in Italy. Members of the Italian parliament and government were under constant pressure from the agricultural organizations to protect their fruit and vegetable production. In a country where the agricultural organizations constituted a formidable voting force, it is hardly surprising that members of parliament and the government were prepared to go to considerable lengths in the Council of Ministers of the European Communities to hold up negotiation of agreements inimical to the interests of their constituencies.

Only when the negotiation of the Maghreb association agreements was viewed from a third perspective (elite networks), did it become clear why, despite all the in-fighting in the Council of Ministers, despite all the popular anti-Arab pressure from the Netherlands, and despite all the organized pressure from the groups representative of fruit- and vegetable-growing interests in Italy, the agreements were finally signed and ratified. This third analysis suggested that the agreements were concluded and signed largely because, on the one hand, a small group of high-level officials responsible for Mediterranean policy in the EEC Commission's directorate general for external relations had been working on the preparation of the agreements for years and had a certain vested interest in seeing their efforts come to fruition. On the other hand, the Permanent Representatives of Morocco and Tunisia to the European Communities engaged in a well-planned joint public relations campaign and were able to ingratiate themselves with some of the noncommitted Community ministers, particularly the Belgian foreign minister. In addition, the Moroccan and Tunisian ambassadors were well-known and well-liked by a small group of officials in D.G. I , partly because a number of them were formerly officials in the French ministries dealing with the overseas countries and had already developed cordial working relationships with the Maghreb diplomats. It was thus possible, in the concluding months of the negotiations, for the D.G. I officials to go ahead drafting the agreements almost under their own steam and turn a blind eye to minor and, at times, major inconsistencies or loopholes.

The decision to introduce an economic and monetary union in the Community presented a really strong case for an exclusively intergovernmental politics interpretation of decision-making in the European Community. No provision was made in the Rome Treaty for any common EEC policies in the area. Only coordination between the member states was provided for. As a result, a whole series of intergovernmental bodies was created to deal with economic and monetary difficulties that arose between the member states. Even when it became eminently clear by the mid-1960s that in the modern economic and monetary system it was inevitable that events in one member country would affect the others, and that something more than simple coordination of policies was necessary, it required a summit conference of the six heads of state (The Hague, December 1969) to give the green light to the creation of an economic and monetary union in the Community. Moreover, the group chiefly responsible for drafting plans for the union was an ad hoc committee drawn from the various intergovernmental committees of the Community and chaired by the Luxembourg minister (both prime minister and minister of finance) who gave the Werner group its name.

The Hague summit conference in December 1969 marked a high point in the resurgence of the "Community spirit" of the late 1960s. In the minds of all those who had been working to strengthen the European Community over the years, it was associated with a renewal of that "political will" referred to by officials, politicians and statesmen as the prerequisite for a more integrated Europe. The final communiqué from The Hague represented a kind of statement of faith and good intentions for the decade of the seventies, and a declaration that the Community planned to work toward the creation of an economic and monetary union by the end of that decade was one of the key points of the communiqué.

Inclusion of the economic and monetary union in the final communiqué of The Hague summit meeting greatly reduced opposition to it from representative groups and the public, as few of the representative groups were willing to lay themselves open to the accusation that they were betraying the idea of greater European integration. Consequently, although some of the largest of the groups, particularly the labor unions, were lukewarm to a scheme that almost inevitably meant strengthening big business and that made remarkably little provision for protecting the interests of labor, they could not afford to dissociate themselves from the "spirit of The Hague." Intentionally or not, the inclusion of the economic and monetary union declaration in the final communiqué of The Hague summit meeting gained support for the scheme from business, industrial, and commercial groups and very effectively defused the opposition of those groups most likely to come out against it. We thus find one of the few examples of almost unanimous public and group support for a project sponsored by the member governments. Under other circumstances and at another time a proposal of such complexity could well have dragged on for years (as, for example, the Mansholt plan to reform agricultural structures in the Community). Instead, the economic and monetary union proposals passed the Council of Ministers in record time.

The composition of the Werner group provides an interesting link between the intergovernmental politics and the elite networks approaches, and also an excellent alternative explanation of why the Community was able to forge ahead and produce highly complex short-, medium- and long-term plans in record time and with the unanimous backing of all the members of the group. This does not mean, of course, that the representatives of the member governments did not have their fights before the proposals for the union were finally approved by the Council of Ministers in February 1971; quite the contrary. Nevertheless, the very fact that the Werner group was composed of men who had learned to know each other very well indeed over the years by sitting on the same committees, attending the same meetings both in EEC institutions and elsewhere, who had in fact learned to work together well before the Werner group brought them together more than twice a month in person, and countless times by telephone, is quite significant. They were men of similar background who had at their disposal a technical expertise that made them into a European Community elite and an international elite at one and the same time.

The important part played by elite networks of all kinds also emerges from an analysis of the free movement of labor decision. In some respects this case bears a resemblance to the agricultural structures decision. In both case studies, an intergovernmental politics approach provides a fairly convincing case for the primacy of national interests in European Community affairs. However, when the free movement of labor decision was viewed from a pluralist perspective it became apparent, just as it became apparent in the agricultural structures decision, that one group of representatives — the Social Affairs Committee of the European Parliament—set out to adopt an independent line. From the introduction of the first measures to free movement of labor in the Community, the parliamentary committee followed closely the work of the EEC Commission and the Council of Ministers in the area, offered both solicited and unsolicited advice, and did everything in its power to push through the necessary measures with all possible speed.

Although the Social Affairs Committee of the European Parliament exerted quite strong pressures on the EEC Commission and the member governments, the zeal of the EEC commissioner responsible for social affairs, Lionello Levi Sandri, must also be taken into account. Commissioner Levi Sandri's energy and persistance was rivaled only by that of Mr. Mansholt in the history of European Community policy-making. Commissioner Levi Sandri also toured the member countries and spoke to varied audiences to plead the cause of harmonizing national social policies in the

European Community. At this point, however, the comparison with Commissioner Mansholt ended. Despite Mr. Levi Sandri's energy and enthusiasm, there were few indications that he was able to attract the same loyal and devoted following among colleagues and aides as did Mr. Mansholt.

If Mr. Levi Sandri did not act as a focus of the same kind of elite network in the EEC Commission as Mr. Mansholt, there is some evidence to suggest that strong affinities existed between the commissioner and his executive aides on the one hand and a powerful nucleus of Italian socialists and former labor union officials in the European Parliament on the other. Mr. Levi Sandri, before his appointment to the EEC Commission, had been actively associated with the Italian Social Democrat party and with its leadership. In addition, he had served at one time as head of the executive staff of the Italian minister of labor and also had sat on a large number of international committees dealing with labor law, social security, and related problems. Thus, from the time of his appointment to the European Commission in 1961, and even more so after he became a vice-president in 1964, Mr. Levi Sandri was in an excellent position to know well and work in close collaboration with leading labor and socialist representatives not only in the European Parliament but also in other European Community bodies, such as the Economic and Social Committee.

As this study has progressed, it has become increasingly clear that the three approaches to decision-making are obviously not exclusive alternatives. Each magnifies certain factors and leaves others out. Each approach, by concentrating on a specific set of variables, naturally pushes other important factors into the background temporarily. Notwithstanding, there are certain links between the approaches. Processes in one tend to affect processes in the others.

The most important link to emerge from the present research was the capacity of individuals and small groups to influence decisions. This feature, until very recently, has been virtually ignored by students of international relations.[4] It has, however, been given some attention by analysts of American foreign policy, such as Graham Allison and Richard Barnet. In his recent *Roots of War*, Barnet analyzes the American national security bureaucracy in terms of the "men and institutions behind U.S. foreign policy."[5] According to one of his reviewers: "The elite [the national security managers] is cohesive, remarkably small, and vigorously self-perpetuating . . . the highest virtue is loyalty to the team. . . . Criticisms are made from within; linen is never washed in public."[6]

With very little rewording, this description could easily apply to the "preferentialists" in the EEC Commission's directorate general for external relations. It could also fit quite comfortably the small group of EEC Commission negotiators, also from D.G. I, who handled the drafting of the

Maghreb association treaties. It could even fit the members of the Werner group. When members of these various elites were interviewed, they first gave the impression that operations ran very smoothly. After futher questioning, they were prepared to admit that there had been internal squabbles and personality clashes, but, they hastened to add, these had been quickly overcome. Only when these interviews were cross-checked, and outsiders were questioned, did it became apparent that the inside group seemed to be making a conscious effort to give the impression of homogeneity and like-mindedness in order to preserve its capacity to influence decisions.

A considerable body of literature on decision-making in the European Community asserts that there is a special way of influencing decisions in the EEC. According to these observers, there is a special system of bargaining, negotiating, coalition formation, and conflict resolution exclusive to its institutions. Lindberg and Scheingold are quite explicit about this: "The Commission and the Council," they write, "have evolved the unique decision-making style that we have called 'the Community method' or the 'Community procedural code.'"[7] David Coombes also asserts that there is a special Community bargaining procedure with its own inherent characteristics:

One essential procedure is the tying together of decisions on different aspects of policy so that they are taken simultaneously as part of a "package deal." . . . This principle of the "package deal" informs most aspects of the work of the Community. . . . Secondly, there is the tactic of settling disputes by agreeing to postpone decisions in the hope that a more favourable time will be found in the future. . . . Both the principle of the "package deal" and the tactic of postponing decisions form part of the Community central strategy, which is the deliberate engineering of regular crises. Much of the life and work of the Commission is now geared to the famous "Community cycle," according to which major decisions tend to be taken all together in great marathon sessions of the Council of Ministers in December of each year, and then again, but to a lesser extent, at the end of June and early July.[8]

This study has revealed that just as there is not one process but many different processes of decision-making in the European Community, so there is not just one method but many different methods of influencing decisions. Just as the processes, the methods will depend on many variables. For the purpose of clarity, they may be grouped into two broad categories: positive methods, such as proposing compromises, building up package deals, and submitting alternatives; negative methods, such as underscoring differences, cutting off options, eliminating alternatives and intensifying conflicts. It is suggested that the tactics used by Community decision-makers are by no means the standard operating procedures that Lindberg, Scheingold, and Coombes claim. Just as the activity of small groups turned out to be crucial, so the personality of decision-makers, the patterns of leadership established, and the techniques of group management employed must be taken into consideration in the analysis. As Allison pointed out in his Cuban missile crisis study: ''Additional paradigms focusing, for example, on individual cognitive processes, or the psychology of central players . . . must be considered.''[9] This study, rather than develop additional paradigms along the lines suggested by Allison, attempted to include, admittedly in a sketchy fashion, a discussion of the behavior of the chief players in each of the five cases.

Much has been written on the difficulties inevitably encountered when the motivations of individuals and small groups are examined. Ways have, however, been suggested of getting round the problem. Philip E. Jacob, in his study of the influence of values in political integration, points out that there are three possible ways of getting out of the difficulty. First, an indicator may be obtained, he suggests, from ''expressions and reflections made privately to 'in-groups' or shared with an interviewer who establishes a relationship of confidence.'' Second, it is possible to compare public statements made to different audiences and see if they are largely consistent with one another. Finally, Jacob suggests, if a study is made of

the histories of particularly difficult or critical decisions. . . . Where material is available describing from the inception of the decisional crisis to its conclusion the conflicts of values which were involved, very real insight can be gained both as to the character of the values at work and changes occurring in the relative weight of the different values.[10]

This study attempted to follow all three research methods suggested by Jacob. In so doing, valuable information was obtained about the relationships between different types of decision-making styles and processes.

It is not suggested here that it is possible to measure the effect of personality variables on group action. There will always be the complex mix of rationality and nonrationality in decision-making. In other words, as Sidney Verba has pointed out, the individual may well assume that he is responding to an event on the basis of a cool and clear-headed means-end calculation. But how do we connect the nonlogical influences on political decisions (those influences acting upon the decision-maker of which he is unaware and which he would not consider a legitimate influence upon his decision if he were aware) with the observable, logical influences?[11] This problem is almost insurmountable. Nonetheless, it has been established that political figures do indeed ''bring to their jobs a set of attitudes, predispositions, ways of looking at the world which, along with such traditionally recognized influences as party, executive leadership and lobby pressures, affect the way they speak and act.''[12] It is the attitudes, predispositions, and ways of looking at the world of the men involved in decision-making in the European Community which seem to have emerged in this study as an important linkage factor between the different "types" of decision-making highlighted in the three conceptual schemes sketched out in the introduction.

Notes

Chapter 1
Decision-Making in the EEC: A Definitional Problem

1. Ernst B. Haas, "The Study of Regional Integration: Reflections on the Joy and Anguish of Pretheorizing," *International Organization* 24, no. 4 (Autumn 1970): 621. Hereafter, Haas, *International Organization* (Autumn 1970).

2. According to Part Five, Articles 137-198 of the treaty, decisions are taken on the basis of proposals initiated by the EEC Commission and submitted to the Council of Ministers, generally after consulting the European Parliament and the Economic and Social Committee of the Communities.

3. Graham T. Allison, "Conceptual Models and the Cuban Missile Crisis," *The American Political Science Review* 63, no. 3: 689-90.

4. Probably the foremost exponent of this approach is Stanley Hoffman in his frequently cited article "Obstinate or Obsolete? The Fate of the Nation-State and the Case of Western Europe," *Daedalus* 95, no. 3 (Summer 1966).

5. Stanley Hoffman in *Gulliver's Troubles, or the Setting of American Foreign Policy* (New York: McGraw Hill, 1968, p. 405) goes even further and equates low politics with harmony and cooperation and high politics with discord and conflict. This leads him to the conclusion that "a formidable resilient barrier continues to close the political kingdom to the Common Market."

6. Karl W. Deutsch, *The Analysis of International Relations* (Englewood Cliffs, N. J.: Prentice Hall, 1968), pp. 103-104.

7. James N. Rosenau, *Public Opinion and Foreign Policy* (New York: Random House, 1961), p. 37 quotes Gabriel A. Almond, "Public Opinion and National Security Policy," *Public Opinion Quarterly* 20 (Summer 1956): 376.

8. Walter Yondorf in "Monnet and the Action Committee: The Formative Period of the European Communities," *International Organization* 19, no. 4 (1965): 887 points out how a network of close ties developed between the originators of the Schuman Plan:

Checking into the history of the nine key men involved, one finds that five held top positions in the Free French Movement during the war. Monnet, Schuman, Mayer, and Pleven were ministers in de Gaulle's Committee of National Liberation in Algiers, and Bidault headed the National Council of Resistance in occupied France from 1943 on. This common background naturally bound these men together.

9. Haas, *International Organization* (Autumn 1970), p. 643.

10. Philip E. Jacob, "The Influence of Values in Political Integration," in Philip E. Jacob and James V. Toscano (eds.) *The Integration of Political Communities* (Philadelphia and New York: J. B. Lippincott Company, 1964), p. 217.

11. Robert William Russell, "A Preliminary Assessment of Small Group Behavior in the International Monetary Circus," Paper presented to a seminar of the Transnational Relations Study Group, Center for International Affairs, Harvard University, October 26, 1972, p. 9. Reprinted with permission.

Chapter 2
The Five Decisions: The Case Histories

1. Commission of the European Communities, Spokesman's Group, *Information Memo P-17* (Brussels, June 1971), p. 2.

2. United Nations Conference on Trade and Development, Document E/CONF.46/L.28 (Geneva, June 16, 1964), p. 72.

3. *Information Memo* P-17, p. 2.

4. European Economic Community, Official Spokesman of the Commission, *Information Memo P-65/66* (Brussels, November 1966) p. 3.

5. European Parliament, *Report on preparations for the second session of the United Nations Conference on Trade and Development*, Document 177, January 19, 1966, p. 11.

6. "Tariff Preferences for the Developing Countries," *European Community*, April 1969 (Washington, European Community Information Service), p. 8.

7. *European Community*, July-August 1971 (Washington: European Community Information Service), pp. 12-24.

8. *Treaty Establishing the European Economic Community and Connected Documents* (Luxembourg: Publishing Services of the European Communities, 1962), p. 57. (Hereafter cited as *Rome Treaty*.)

9. Commission of the European Communities, Spokesman's Group, *Information Memo P-16* (Brussels, March 1969).

10. *Rome Treaty*, p. 163.

11. *Treaty Establishing the European Coal and Steel Community* (Luxembourg: High Authority of the European Coal and Steel Community, 1951), pp. 47-48. Article 69 reads:

1. The member States bind themselves to renounce any restriction, based on

nationality, on the employment in the coal and steel industries of workers of recognized qualifications for positions in such industries possessing the nationality of one of the member States; this commitment shall be subject to the limitations imposed by the fundamental needs of health and public order. . . .

4. They will prohibit any discrimination in payment and working conditions as between national and foreign workers, without prejudice to special measures concerning frontier workers; in particular, they will work out among themselves any arrangements necessary so that social security measures do not stand in the way of the movement of labour. . . .

12. *Rome Treaty*, p. 57.

13. European Economic Community, Commission, Official Spokesman's Group, *Information Memo P-5410* (Brussels, June 12, 1961).

14. European Economic Community, Official Spokesman of the Commission, *Information Memo P-20/64* (Brussels, April 1964).

15. Commission of the European Communities, Spokesman's Group, *Information Memo P-50-68* (Brussels, July 1968).

16. *Rome Treaty*, Article 39, paragraph 1, reads:

(a) to increase agricultural productivity by developing technical progress and by ensuring the rational development of agricultural production and the optimum utilisation of the factors of production, particularly labour;

(b) to ensure thereby a fair standard of living for the agricultural population, particularly by the increasing of the individual earnings of persons engaged in agriculture;

(c) to stabilize markets;

(d) to guarantee regular supplies; and

(e) to ensure reasonable prices in supplies to consumers.

17. "Decision Concerning the Co-ordination of Policies on Agricultural Structure" (Proposal of the Commission to the Council) *Bulletin of the EEC Commission*, 1962, No. 3-Supplement (Brussels: Publishing Services of the European Communities, 1962), p. 1.

18. Ibid., p. 2.

19. "Décision du Conseil en date du 4 décembre 1962 concernant la coordination des politiques de structure agricole," *Journal Officiel des Communautés Européennes*, 17 décembre 1962 (Brussels: Publishing Services of the European Communities), pp. 2892-95.

20. "Proposal for a Council Regulation on the European Fund for Structural Improvements in Agriculture," *Bulletin of the EEC Commission* 1963, No. 4-Supplement (Brussels: Publishing Services of the European Communities), pp. 4-11.

21. *European Community*, No. 145, May 1971 (Washington: European Community Information Service), p. 3.

22. *European Community*, June 1970 (London: European Community Information Service), p. 3.

23. ECSC-EEC-EAEC, Secretariat General of the Commission, *Bulletin no. 4-1971 of the European Communities* (Brussels: Publishing Services of the European Communities, 1971), p. 59.

24. *European Community*, No. 145, May 1971 (Washington: European Community Information Service), pp. 3-4.

25. *Rome Treaty*, Article 2:

It shall be the aim of the Community, by establishing a Common Market and progressively approximating the economic policies of Member States, to promote throughout the Community a harmonious development of economic activities, a continuous and balanced expansion, an increased stability, an accelerated raising of the standard of living and closer relations between its Member States.

Article 6 reads:

1. Member States, acting in close collaboration with the institutions of the Community, shall coordinate their respective economic policies to the extent that is necessary to attain the objectives of this Treaty. . . .

26. *Rome Treaty*, Articles 103, 105 and 107.

27. European Economic Community, Official Spokesman of the Commission, *Information Memo P-59/64* (Brussels: October 1964), pp. 4-5.

28. European Economic Community. *Tenth General Report on the Activities of the Community*, 1 April 1966-31 March 1967 (Brussels: June 1967), pp. 164-65.

29. European Coal and Steel Community, European Economic Community, European Atomic Energy Community. *Second General Report on the Activities of the Community 1968* (Brussels-Luxembourg: February 1969), p. 111.

30. ECSC-EEC-EAEC, Secretariat General of the Commission. *Commission Memorandum to the Council on the Co-ordination of Economic Policies and Monetary Co-operation within the Community* (Supplement to Bulletin No. 3-1969 of the European Communities) (Brussels: Publishing Services of the European Communities, 1969).

31. European Coal and Steel Community, European Economic Community, European Atomic Energy Community, *Third General Report on the Activities of the Communities 1969* (Brussels-Luxembourg, February 1970), p. 488.

32. ECSC-EEC-EAEC, Secretariat General of the Commission. *Bulletin No. 5-1970 of the European Communities* (Brussels: Publishing Services of the European Communities, 1970), p. 50.

33. European Community Information Service, Washington. Press release, August 6, 1971.

34. Ibid.

Chapter 3
Generalized Preferences

1. C.E.E. Porte-parole de la Commission, Note 14589, February 1964.

2. European Economic Community, Official Spokesman of the Commission, *Press Release* IP (64) 62, Brussels, March 17, 1964.

3. *Journal Officiel des Communautés Européennes,* November 6, 1964, pp. 2803-2804. Author's translation.

4. Communauté Economique Européenne, Commission: "Octroi de préférences tarifaires par les pays industrialisés aux produits semi-finis et finis de l'ensemble des pays en voie de développement" (Communication de la Commission au Conseil) SEC (66) 3585 final, Brussels, November 22, 1966.

5. Question écrite no. 161 de M. Pedini à la Commission de la Communauté économique européenne. Brussels, April 30, 1965. Author's translation.

6. Communauté Economique Européenne: Le Conseil. Note d'information: "Travaux du Comité Spécial des Préférences de l'U.N.C.T.A.D." (New York, 10-28 mai 1965), B/640/65 (COMER 96), Brussels, June 15, 1965, pp. 3-7.

7. Personal interviews, Brussels, March 1972.

8. EUROPE Bulletin, November 27, 1965.

9. *Journal of Commerce*, December 30, 1966.

10. EUROPE Bulletin, December 7, 1967.

11. European Parliament: Working Documents 1967-1968. Report drawn up on behalf of the Committee on External Trade Relations on preparations for the second session of the United Nations Conference on Trade and Development. Document 177, January 19, 1968, Rapporteur Mr. Pedini. Unofficial English translation, p. 3.

12. Parlement Européen: Documents de Séance 1968-1969. Rapport fait au nom de la commission des relations économiques extérieures sur les résultats de la deuxième session de la Conférence des Nations Unies sur le commerce et le développement. Document 86, July 1, 1968, Rapporteur: Mr. Pedini. p. 12. Author's translation.

13. *Journal of Commerce*, January 30, 1968.

14. Commission of the European Communities, Directorate General for Overseas Development, Interoffice memo, January 1969.

15. Commission of the European Communities, Executive Secretariat, note, March 1969.

16. Personal interviews, Brussels, February and March 1972.

17. Ibid.

18. Committee of Permanent Representatives of the European Communities, note, November 5, 1970.

19. Union des Industries de la Communauté Européenne, "Octroi éventuel de préférences tarifaires pour les produits manufacturés et semi-manufacturés des pays en voie de développement," Brussels, January 24, 1968. Author's translation.

20. Ibid. Author's translation.

21. Bureau de liaison des Industries de Caoutchouc de la Communauté économique européenne, "L'octroi éventuel de préférences tarifaires aux pays en voie de développement," Brussels, November 8, 1968. Author's translation.

22. Letters from the Fédération Européenne de la Ganterie de Peau, November 21, 1968 and from the Syndicat Général des Fabricants de Ficelles, Cordages et Filets, November 25, 1968.

23. EUROPE Bulletin, February 18, 1969. Original translation. Reprinted with permission.

24. Union des Industries de la Communauté Européenne, "Octroi de préférences tarifaires généralisées pour les exportations de produits manufacturés et semi-manufacturés des pays en voie de développement," Brussels, February 27, 1969. Author's translation.

25. Council of the European Communities, press release, March 4, 1969.

26. EUROPE Bulletin, June 15, 1970.

27. EUROPE Bulletin, October 2, 1970. Reprinted with permission.

28. Ibid. Emphasis in the original.

29. Written question No. 208/70 by Mr. Spénale to the Commission of the European Communities, November 5, 1970.

30. EUROPE Bulletin, April 7, 1971.

31. Letter to EEC Commission President Malfatti from the Commission Inter-professionnelle des Industries de l'Habillement de la CEE, May 5, 1971. Author's translation; and EUROPE Bulletin, May 26, 1971.

32. Parlement Européen: Documents de Séance 1971-1972. Rapport fait au nom de la commission des relations économiques extérieures sur les propositions de la Commission des Communautés européennes au Conseil

(doc. 65/71) relatives à des règlements et des décisions concernant la mise en oeuvre des préférences généralisées en faveur des pays en voie de développement. Document 71/71, June 9, 1971. Rapporteur: Mr. T. Westerterp, p. 8. Author's translation.

33. EUROPE Bulletin, June 9, 1971.

34. European Economic Community, Official Spokesman of the Commission, *Press Release* IP (64) 62, Brussels, March 17, 1964.

35. Personal interviews, Brussels, February and March 1972.

36. Ibid.

37. Ibid.

38. Ibid.

39. Ibid.

40. Ibid.

41. Ibid.

42. Ibid.

43. Inter-office memorandum, Directorate general for overseas development, June 1966. Author's translation.

44. Committee of Permanent Representatives of the European Communities, June 10, 1971. Author's translation.

Chapter 4
The Maghreb Association Agreements

1. EUROPE Bulletin, April 9, 1965. Emphasis in the original, Reprinted with permission.

2. Ibid.

3. Ibid.

4. *Opera Mundi*, September 21, 1967.

5. Personal interview, March 1972.

6. *Opera Mundi*, August 8, 1968, pp. 13-14.

7. European Parliament Secretariat, General Directorate of Parliamentary Documentation and Information, *European Documentation: A Survey*, 1968, no. 4, pp. 73-74. Hereafter cited as *European Documentation*.

8. Personal interviews, February and March 1972.

9. *Opera Mundi*, July 21, 1966.

10. *Opera Mundi*, August 8, 1968, pp. 13-14.

11. *European Documentation*, 1968, no. 4, pp. 73-74.

12. Ibid., 1969, no. 2, pp. 78-79.

13. Ibid.

14. EUROPE Bulletin, December 19, 1968.

15. Parlement Européen Documents de Séance 1968-1969, Proposition de résolution présentée par MM. Metzger, Vals, Wohlfart, Vredeling et Dehousse au nom du groupe socialiste sur la politique de la Communauté à l'égard du bassin méditerranéen. Document 202, January 23, 1969.

16. EUROPE Bulletin, February 21, 1969.

17. *European Parliament: Document 48, Bersani Report*, p. 17.

18. Ibid., p. 24.

19. Personal interview, Brussels, March 1972.

20. Ibid.

21. Commission des communautés européennes, Groupe du Porte-parole, Note, Brussels, November 27, 1968. Author's translation.

22. Ibid.

23. Personal interview, Brussels, March 1972.

24. Rabat and Tunis Treaties, Article 14, paragraph 2.

25. Personal interview, Brussels, March 1972.

Chapter 5
Free Movement of Labor

1. "Free Movement of Workers in the European Community," *Bulletin of the European Communities*, 1968, no. 11, pp. 5-9.

2. Cormac O'Grada, "The Vocational Training Policy of the EEC and the Free Movement of Skilled Labour," *Journal of Common Market Studies*, 8 (December 1969): 87.

3. "The Role of Social Policy in European Integration." Address by M. Levi Sandri, member of the EEC Commission, to the General Meeting of the Belgian Association for Social Progress, February 10, 1964. (Hereafter cited as Levi Sandri speech, February 1964.)

4. European Parliament, Secretariat, General Directorate of Parliamentary Documentation and Information, *European Documentation: A Survey*, 1967, no. 1, p. 53.

5. Parlement Européen, Direction Générale de la Documentation Parlementaire et de l'Information. Communiqué de presse. Brussels, November 3, 1967. Author's translation.

6. Assemblée Parlementaire Européenne, Documents de Séance 1960-61, Rapport sur le règlement relatif aux premières mesures pour la

réalisation de la libre circulation des travailleurs dans la Communauté. Document 67, Octobre 1960, Rapporteur: M.L. Rubinacci, p. 2. (Hereafter cited as European Parliament Document 67: Rubinacci Report.) Author's translation.

7. "Guidelines for the EEC Commission's Work in the Social Sector" (Memorandum submitted by the Commission to the Council on 22 December 1966), *Supplement to the Bulletin of the European Communities,* 1967, no. 2, p. 7.

8. *Journal Officiel des Communautés Européennes,* December 7, 1967, no. 298, p. 14. Author's translation.

9. "Free Movement of Workers in the European Community," *Bulletin of the European Communities,* 1968, no. 11, pp. 5-9.

10. European Parliament Document 67: Rubinacci Report, p. 1. Author's translation.

11. Assemblée Parlementaire Européenne, Documents de Séance 1961-1962. Rapport complémentaire sur le règlement relatif aux premières mesures pour la réalisation de la libre circulation des travailleurs dans la Communauté. Document 86, 13 novembre 1961, p. 2. Rapporteur M. Rubinacci. (Hereafter cited as European Parliament Document 86: Rubinacci Report.) Author's translation.

12. Ibid., p. 3.

13. Ibid., p. 6. Author's translation.

14. EUROPE Bulletin, July 25, 1968; July 29, 1968; July 30, 1968.

15. Personal interview, March 1972.

16. European Parliament Document 67: Rubinacci Report, p. 1.

17. *Journal Officiel des Communautés Européennes,* 16 novembre 1960, p. 1389. Author's translation.

18. European Parliament Document 86: Rubinacci Report, p. 1. Author's translation.

19. Question écrite No. 97/1961-1962 by Mr. Nederhorst to the Commission of the European Economic Community, March 22, 1962.

20. European Economic Community, Official Spokesman of the Commission, *Information Memo P-16(64)* (Brussels: March 1964).

21. EUROPE Bulletin, April 13, 1967.

22. Parlement Européen, Documents de Séance 1967-68. Rapport sur les propositions de la Commission de la C.E.E. au Conseil d'un règlement relatif à la libre circulation des travailleurs à l'intérieur de la Communauté, d'une directive relative à la suppression des restrictions au déplacement et au séjour des travailleurs des Etats membres et de leur famille à l'intérieur de la Communauté. Document 128, 10 octobre 1967, p. 41. Rapporteur: M. Pêtre. Author's translation.

23. European Parliament Document 67: Rubinacci Report, p. 10. Author's translation.

24. Levi Sandri speech, February 1964, p. 6.

25. "Social Policy and Medium-Term Economic Policy," extracts from address by M. Levi Sandri, Vice-President of the EEC Commission, at the 49th International Labour Conference, Geneva, 11 June 1965. European Economic Community, Official Spokesman of the Commission, *Press Release IP (65) 109,* June 10, 1965.

26. EUROPE Bulletin, July 29, 1968.

27. Personal interview, March 1972.

28. Levi Sandri speech, February 1964.

29. All biographical data were obtained from the annual yearbooks of the European Parliament.

30. Personal interviews, March 1972.

Chapter 6
Agricultural Structures

1. *Le Monde*, December 12, 1968. Author's translation.

2. *Christian Science Monitor*, February 5, 1969.

3. *Opera Mundi*, January 30, 1919, pp. 2-3.

4. EUROPE Bulletin, January 28, 1969.

5. Ibid.

6. *European Documentation*, 1968, no. 4, p. 53.

7. EUROPE Bulletin, July 7, 1969.

8. *Opera Mundi*, June 26, 1969, pp. 8-9.

9. EUROPE Bulletin, May 13, 1969.

10. Ibid., September 26, 1969.

11. Ibid., May 8, 1970.

12. *Opera Mundi*, February 5, 1970, p. 3.

13. *European Community*, European Community Information Service, Washington, No. 145, May 1971, pp. 3-4.

14. EUROPE Bulletin, February 16, 1971.

15. Ibid., March 17, 1971.

16. *European Documentation*, 1971, No. 1, pp. 65-66.

17. EUROPE Bulletin, March 25, 1971. Reprinted with permission.

18. *Süddeutsche Zeitung*, December 12, 1968.

19. "Les Réactions au Plan Mansholt," Etude et Analyses, Commis-

sion des Communautés Européennes, Direction Générale Presse et Information, January 1969, p. 4-5. (Hereafter cited as "Les Réactions au Plan Mansholt.").

20. *Le Monde*, December 15, 1968.

21. *Süddeutsche Zeitung,* December 17, 1968.

22. "Les Réactions au Plan Mansholt," pp. 8-9.

23. Ibid., p. 6.

24. *24 Ore,* January 24, 1969.

25. "Les Réactions au Plan Mansholt," p. 7.

26. *Le Monde*, January 12, 1969. Author's translation.

27. *Opera Mundi*, March 13, 1969.

28. Bulletin de la Fédération des Industries belges, No. 26, 1969.

29. Confédération Européenne des Syndicats Libres dans la Communauté, Organisation Européenne de la C.M.T. Communiqué à la presse. "Des comités executifs prennent position sur le 'Mémorandum 1980.'" Brussels, October 17, 1969.

30. EUROPE Bulletin, January 8, 1970.

31. Commission of the European Communities, Monthly Bulletin, 1970, no. 5, p. 110.

32. Ibid., p. 122.

33. EUROPE Bulletin, April 9, 1970.

34. Commission of the European Communities, Monthly Bulletin, 1970, no. 7, p. 118 (May 23, 1970).

35. *European Documentation*, 1970, no. 3, pp. 94-97.

36. EUROPE Bulletin, October 16, 1970.

37. Ibid., January 11, 1971.

38. Commission of the European Communities, Monthly Bulletin, 1971, no. 4, pp. 155-156 (February 11, 1971).

39. EUROPE Bulletin, February 15, 1971.

40. Ibid., February 17, 1971.

41. Ibid., March 8, 1971.

42. Ibid., March 18, 1971.

43. Comité des Organisations Professionnelles Agricoles de la C.E.E. (C.O.P.A.). "Résolution de l'Assemblée générale extraordinaire," Brussels, March 23, 1971. Author's translation.

44. "EEC-wide farm policy may halt national twists," John Lambert in the *Christian Science Monitor*, April 3, 1971. Reprinted by permission from the *Christian Science Monitor*, © 1971 The Christian Science Publishing Society. All rights reserved.

45. Personal interviews; Brussels, February and March 1972.

46. Ibid.

47. Ibid.

48. Commission of the EEC, Information memo, April 1959. Author's translation.

49. Personal interviews, Brussels, February and March 1972.

50. Ibid.

51. Ibid.

52. *Financial Times*, May 22, 1970. Reprinted with permission.

53. Ibid., December 12 and 20, 1968.

54. *European Documentation*, 1969, no. 1, p. 1.

55. *Le Monde*, January 9, 1969.

56. EUROPE Bulletin, January 21, 1969.

57. *European Documentation*, 1969, no. 1, p. 134.

58. *Le Monde*, March 22, 1969.

59. Ibid., July 27, 1969.

60. Personal interview, Brussels, March 1972.

61. Ibid.

62. Ibid.

63. Ibid.

64. Ibid.

65. Commission of the European Communities, Spokesman's Group, *Press Release* IP (71) 63, Brussels, March 31, 1971.

66. Personal interview, Brussels, February 1972.

67. EUROPE Bulletin, September 29, 1970 and *Le Monde*, September 30, 1970.

68. EUROPE Bulletin, March 1, 1971.

69. *Christian Science Monitor*, April 3, 1971.

70. EUROPE Bulletin, January 25, 1971.

Chapter 7
Economic and Monetary Union

1. Commission of the European Communities, *Monthly Bulletin*, 1971, no. 3, p. 97.

2. *European Documentation, A Survey,* European Parliament Secretariat, General Directorate of Parliamentary Documentation, 1970, no. 2, pp. 7-8 (hereafter cited as *European Documentation*).

3. Ibid., pp. 43-44.

4. *European Documentation,* 1970, no. 4, pp. 50-52.

5. Commission of the European Communities, *Monthly Bulletin,* 1970 no. 4, p. 105.

6. EUROPE Bulletin, April 21, 1969.

7. Ibid., July 16, 1969.

8. Ibid., July 18, 1969.

9. *Opera Mundi,* January 29, 1970.

10. *European Documentation,* 1970, no. 2, p. 71.

11. Ibid.

12. *Opera Mundi,* June 4, 1970.

13. EUROPE Bulletin, June 9, 1970.

14. *Opera Mundi,* October 15, 1970.

15. Ibid., November 12, 1970.

16. Ph. Lemaître, *Le Monde,* November 25, 1970. Author's translation. Reprinted with permission.

17. Ibid., November 24, 1970. Author's translation. Reprinted with permission.

18. EUROPE Bulletin, December 15, 1970.

19. Ibid., February 5, 1971.

20. *New York Times,* February 10, 1971.

21. Personal interview, March 1972.

22. Address by M. Raymond Barre, Vice-President of the Commission of the European Communities, at the Fifth International Investment Symposium, Bellagio, June 2, 1970, p. 13.

23. Personal interview, Brussels, March 1972.

24. *European Documentation,* 1970, no. 4, pp. 197-200.

25. EUROPE Bulletin, September 21, 1970 and *European Documentation,* 1970, no. 3, pp. 109-113.

26. *European Documentation,* 1971, no. 1, pp. 161-163.

27. EUROPE Bulletin, September 25, 1969. Reprinted with permission.

28. *European Documentation,* 1970, no. 3, pp. 75-76.

29. Ibid., 1971, no. 1, pp. 140-141.

30. Ibid., 1970, no. 4, pp. 156-157.

31. EUROPE Bulletin, September 23, 1969.

32. Comité Economique et Social, Compte rendu des délibérations, 92ème session plénière, Brussels, February 22, 1971.

33. Personal interview, Brussels, March 1972.

34. Confédération Européenne des Syndicats Libres dans la Communauté, Communiqué à la presse, "Union Economique et monétaire oui, mais avec la participation des travailleurs," Brussels, May 13, 1970. Author's translation.

35. Commission of the European Communities, *Monthly Bulletin*, 1970, no. 5, p. 124.

36. *European Documentation*, 1971, no. 1, p. 127.

37. Personal interview, Brussels, February 1972.

38. Commission of the European Communities, Directorate General for Press and Information, Textes Selectionnées, "Le Plan Werner devant la Presse," Brussels, November 16, 1970.

39. European Economic Community, *Ninth Report on the Activities of the Monetary Committee,* Brussels, Publications Services of the European Communities, March 1967, pp. 11-12.

40. European Communities, Monetary Committee, *Twelfth Report on the Activities of the Monetary Committee,* Brussels, Office for Official Publications of the European Communities, pp. 23-24.

41. Commission of the European Communities, *Monthly Bulletin*, 1970, no. 6, p. 54.

42. *Opera Mundi*, October 1, 1970, pp. 4-5.

43. Personal interviews, Brussels, March 1972.

44. Ibid.

45. Speech by Vice President of the EEC Commission Raymond Barre before the European Parliament, November 18, 1970, cited in Commission of the European Communities, *Monthly Bulletin*, 1971, no. 1, p. 18.

46. *Wall Street Journal*, March 25, 1971. Reprinted with permission.

47. Robert William Russell, "A Preliminary Assessment of Small Group Behavior in the International Monetary Circus." Paper presented to a seminar of the Transnational Relations Study Group, Center for International Affairs, Harvard University, October 26, 1972, p. 2. Reprinted with permission.

48. Ibid.

Chapter 8
Conclusion

1. Leon N. Lindberg, *The Political Dynamics of European Economic Integration* (Stanford: Stanford University Press, 1963).

2. Leon N. Lindberg and Stuart A. Scheingold, *Europe's Would-Be Polity* (Englewood Cliffs, N.J; Prentice-Hall, 1970).

3. Gordon M. Adams, "Political Integration in Europe: The African Association to the European Economic Community," (unpublished Ph.D. dissertation, Department of Political Science, Columbia University, 1971).

4. An exception to this is the work of Robert W. Russell on small group dynamics in the international monetary arena. See his recent article, "Transgovernmental Interaction in the International Monetary System, 1960-1972," *International Organization* 27, no. 4 (Autumn 1973): 431-64.

5. Richard J. Barnet, *Roots of War* (New York: Atheneum, 1972).

6. Ronald Steel, "Roots of War," *New York Times*, June 11, 1972.

7. Lindberg and Scheingold, passim.

8. David Coombes, *Politics and Bureaucracy in the European Community* (Beverly Hills, Calif.: Sage Publications, 1970), pp. 284-86.

9. Graham T. Allison, *Essence of Decision: Explaining the Cuban Missile Crisis* (Boston: Little, Brown and Company, 1971), p. 277.

10. Philip E. Jacob, "The Influence of Values in Political Integration," in Philip E. Jacob and James V. Toscano (eds.) *The Integration of Political Communities* (Philadelphia: J.B. Lippincott Company, 1964), pp. 229-30.

11. Sidney Verba, "Assumptions of Rationality and Non-Rationality in Models of the International System," in Klaus Knorr and Sidney Verba (eds.) *The International System* (Princeton: Princeton University Press, 1961), pp. 94-97.

12. Bruce M. Russett, "International Communication and Legislative Behavior: The Senate and the House of Commons," in Louis Kriesberg (ed.) *Social Processes in International Relations* (New York: John Wiley and Sons, 1968), p. 81.

Bibliography

Books, Articles and Papers

Adams, Gordon M. "Political Integration in Europe: The African Association to the European Economic Community." Unpublished Ph.D. dissertation. Political Science Department, Columbia University, 1971.

Allison, Graham T. "Conceptual Models and the Cuban Missile Crisis." *The American Political Science Review*, vol 63, no. 3.

_____. *Essence of Decision: Explaining the Cuban Missile Crisis*. Boston: Little, Brown and Company, 1971.

Barnet, Richard J. *Roots of War*. New York: Atheneum, 1972.

Cobb, Roger W. and Elder, Charles. *International Community: A Regional and Global Study*. New York: Holt, Rinehart & Winston, 1970.

Common Market Reporter. Chicago and New York: Commerce Clearing House.

Coombes, David. *Politics and Bureaucracy in the European Community: A Portrait of the Commission of the E.E.C.* Beverly Hills, Calif.: Sage Publications, 1970.

Delorme, Hélène and Tavernier, Yves. *Les Paysans Français et l' Europe*. Paris: A. Colin, 1969.

Deutsch, Karl. *The Analysis of International Relations*. Englewood Cliffs, N.J.: Prentice Hall, 1968.

"Les Français et l'Unification Politique de l'Europe d'après un Sondage de la SOFRES." *Revue française de science politique* 19, no. 1 (February 1969): 145-70.

Gerbet, Pierre and Pepy, Daniel. *La Décision dans les Communautés Européennes*. Brussels: Presses Universitaires de Bruxelles, 1969.

Haas, Ernst B. "The Study of Regional Integration: Reflections on the Joy and Anguish of Pretheorizing," *International Organization* 24, no. 4 (Autumn 1970): 607-46.

Hallstein, Walter. *United Europe: Challenge and Opportunity*. London: Oxford University Press, 1962.

Hoffman, Stanley, *Gulliver's Troubles, or the Setting of American Foreign Policy,* New York: McGraw Hill, 1968.

_____. "Obstinate or Obsolete? The Fate of the Nation-State and the Case of Western Europe," in *International Regionalism: Readings*. Edited by Joseph S. Nye, Jr. Boston: Little, Brown and Company, 1968.

Holt, Stephen. *The Common Market: The Conflict of Theory and Practice*. London: Hamish Hamilton, 1967.

155

Inglehart, Ronald. "Cognitive Mobilization and European Identity." *Comparative Politics* 3, no. 1 (October 1970): 45-70.

_____. "An End to European Integration?" *The American Political Science Review* 61, no. 1, March 1967.

_____. "Public Opinion and Regional Integration." *International Organization* 24, no. 4 (Autumn 1970): 764-95.

Jacob, Philip E. and Toscano James V. (Eds.). *The Integration of Political Communities*. Philadelphia and New York: J.P. Lippincott Company, 1964.

Knorr, Klaus and Verba, Sidney (Eds.). *The International System*. Princeton: Princeton University Press, 1961.

Kriesberg, Louis (Ed.). *Social Processes in International Relations*. New York: John Wiley and Sons, 1968.

Lambert, John. "Decision-Making in the Community: The Commission-Council Dialogue." *Government and Opposition* 2, no. 3, (April-July 1967): 391-97.

Lemaignen, R. *L'Europe au Berceau*. Paris: Plon, 1963.

Lindberg, Leon N. "Decision-Making and Integration in the European Community." *International Organization* 19, no. 1 (Winter 1965): 56-80.

_____. *The Political Dynamics of European Economic Integration*. Stanford: Stanford University Press, 1963.

_____. "Political Integration as a Multidimensional Phenomenon Requiring Multivariate Measurement." *International Organization* 24, no. 4 (Autumn 1970): 649-731.

_____. and Scheingold, Stuart A. *Europe's Would-Be Polity*. Englewood Cliffs, N.J.: Prentice-Hall, 1970.

Mayne, Richard. *The Institutions of the European Community*. London: PEP/Chatham House, 1968.

_____. "The Role of Jean Monnet." *Government and Opposition*, 2, no. 3 (April-July 1967): 349-71.

Monnet, Jean. *Les Etats-Unis d'Europe ont Commencé*. Paris: Robert Laffont, 1955.

Niblock, Michael. *The EEC: National Parliaments in Community Decisionmaking*. London: PEP/Chatham House, 1971.

Noel, Emile. "The Committee of Permanent Representatives." *Journal of Common Market Studies* 5, no. 3, (1967): 219-51.

_____. *Institutions Communautaires et Institutions Nationales dans le Dévelopement des Communautés*. Brussels: Institut d'Etudes Européennes, 1968.

_____. and Etienne, H. "Quelques Aspects des Rapports et de la Collaboration entre le Conseil et la Commission." Brussels: Information Service of the European Communities, undated.

O'Grada, Cormac. "The Vocational Training Policy of the EEC and the Free Movement of Skilled Labour." *Journal of Common Market Studies* 8, no. 2 (December 1969): 79-109.

Pignot, P. "Prise de Position des Organisations Professionnelles sur le Mémorandum Concernant la Réforme des Structures Agricoles." *Revue du Marché Commun,* no. 128, numéro spécial, novembre-décembre 1969, pp. 637-642.

Rabier, Jacques-René. *L'Information des Européens et l'Intégration de l'Europe.* Brussels: Institut d'Etudes Européennes, 1965.

———. *L'Opinion Publique et l'Europe.* Brussels: Institut de Sociologie, 1966.

Revue du Marché Commun, numéro spécial, "L'Agriculture Européenne à un Tournant," no. 128, novembre-décembre 1969.

Rosenau, James, N. *Public Opinion and Foreign Policy.* New York: Random House, 1961.

———. (Ed.). *International Politics and Foreign Policy: A Reader in Research and Theory.* Glencoe, Ill.: Free Press, 1961.

Russell, Robert W. "A Preliminary Assessment of Small Group Behavior in the International Monetary Circus." Paper presented to a seminar of the Transnational Relations Study Group, Center for International Affairs, Harvard University, October 26, 1972.

Scheinman, Lawrence. "Some Preliminary Notes on Bureaucratic Relationships in the European Economic Community." *International Organization* 20, no. 4 (Autumn 1966); 750-73.

Snyder, Richard C., Bruck, H.W. and Sapin, Burton. "Motivational Analysis of Foreign Policy Decision-Making." *International Politics and Foreign Policy.* Edited by James N. Rosenau. New York: The Free Press, 1961, pp. 247-253.

———. and Robinson, J. *National and International Decision-Making.* New York: The Institute for International Order, 1961.

Spinelli, Altiero. *The Eurocrats: Conflict and Crisis in the EEC.* Baltimore: The Johns Hopkins Press, 1966.

Université Libre de Bruxelles, Institut d'Etudes Européennes. *Institutions Communautaires et Institutions Nationales dans le Développement des Communautés.* Brussels: Editions de l'Institut de Sociologie, 1968.

Yondorf, Walter. "Monnet and the Action Committee: The Formative Period of the European Communities." *International Organization* 19, no. 4 (Autumn 1965): 885-912.

European Community Documents

European Economic Community—Associated African and Malagasy States, Parliamentary Conference of the Association. *Report drawn up on behalf of the Joint Committee on the second annual report on the activities of the Council of Association (Doc. 9) to the Parliamentary Conference of the Association,* Document 12, November 16, 1966.

European Coal and Steel Community. *Treaty Establishing the European Coal and Steel Community.* High Authority of the European Coal and Steel Community, 1951.

European Economic Community. *Ninth General Report on the Activities of the Community* (1 April 1965-31 March 1966). Brussels, June 1966.

————. *Tenth General Report on the Activities of the Community* (1 April 1966-31 March 1967). Brussels, June 1967.

European Coal and Steel Community, European Economic Community, European Atomic Energy Community. *First General Report on the Activities of the Communities 1967.* Brussels-Luxembourg, February 1968.

————. *Second General Report on the Activities of the Communities 1968.* Brussels-Luxembourg, February 1969.

————. *Third General Report on the Activities of the Communities 1969.* Brussels-Luxembourg, February 1970.

Communauté Européenne du Charbon et de l'Acier, Communauté Economique Européenne, Communauté Européenne de l'Energie Atomique. *Quatrième Rapport Général sur l'Activité des Communautés 1970.* Brussels-Luxembourg, February 1971.

European Economic Community, Commission. "Decision Concerning the Coordination of Policies on Agricultural Structure." Bulletin Supplement, 1962, no. 3.

————. "Memorandum of the Commission on the Action Programme of the Community for the Second Stage," 1962.

————. "Proposal for a Council Regulation on the European Fund for Structural Improvements in Agriculture." Bulletin Supplement, 1963, No. 4.

————. "Octroi des préférences tarifaires par les pays industrialisés aux produits semi-finis et finis de l'ensemble des pays en voie de développement." Document SEC(66)3585. Nov. 22, 1966.

————. "Octroi de préferences aux pays en voie de développement. Quatrième partie: résumé des différentes positions." Bureau de presse et d'information de Genève, 6 février 1967.

_____. "Guidelines for the EEC Commission's Work in the Social Sector." Bulletin Supplement, 1967, No. 2.

_____. "Bibliographie sur la libre circulation des travailleurs à l'intérieur des Communautés Européennes." Document 13309/V/68, October 1968.

_____. "Réactions au mémorandum de la Commission sur la réforme de l'agriculture." Document 12.041/VI/69-F. 1969.

_____. "Les réactions au Plan Mansholt." Etudes et Analyses, Document 1026/X/69-f, January 20, 1969.

_____. "La libre circulation des travailleurs à l'intérieur des Communautés Européennes. Situation au 15 avril 1969." Bibliographie No. 6, Doc. IX/8436/69-f.

_____. "Memorandum on the Reform of Agriculture in the European Economic Community and Annexes." Bulletin Supplement, 1969, No. 1.

_____. "Commission Memorandum to the Council on the Coordination of Economic Policies and Monetary Cooperation within the Community." Bulletin Supplement, 1970, No. 3.

_____. "A Plan for the Phased Establishment of an Economic and Monetary Union." Bulletin Supplement, 1970, No. 3.

_____. "Commission Memorandum and Proposals to the Council on the Establishment by Stages of Economic and Monetary Union." Offprint Bulletin, 1970, No. 11.

_____. "Le Plan Werner devant la Presse." Directorate General for Press and Information, November 16, 1970.

_____. "La mise en application de l'offre de la Communauté en matière de préférences généralisées à octroyer en faveur des exportations d'articles manufacturés et de produits semi-finis des pays en voie de développement." Document SEC(71)1000, March 15, 1971.

_____. "Les Français et leur Agriculture," May 1971.

CEE: CEEA. Comité Economique et Social. "100ème réunion de la Section spécialisée pour l'agriculture, Séance académique." Doc. CP 21/69(460) annexes 1-7, September 16, 1969.

_____. Compte rendu des délibérations, 92ème session plénière, February 22, 1971.

European Economic Community: Council. "Travaux du comité spécial des préférences de l'UNCTAD." Doc. R/640/65 (COMER), June 15, 1965.

European Communities: Council/Commission. "Interim Report on the

Establishment by Stages of Economic and Monetary Union: Werner Report.'' Bulletin Supplement, 1970, No. 1.

———. ''Report to the Council and the Commission on the Realisation by Stages of Economic and Monetary Union in the Community. Werner Report.'' Bulletin Supplement, 1970, no. 11.

European Communities: Monetary Committee. *Twelfth Report on the Activities of the Monetary Committee.*

European Parliament. Rapport sur le règlement relatif aux premières mesures pour la réalisation de la libre circulation des travailleurs dans la Communauté. Doc. 67, October 1960.

———. Rapport complémentaire sur le règlement relatif aux premières mesures pour la réalisation de la libre circulation des travailleurs dans la Communauté. Doc. 86, November 13, 1961.

———. Rapport sur les résultats de la troisième réunion de la conférence parlementaire de l'association. Doc. 16, March 14, 1967.

———. Rapport sur les propositions de la Commission de la C.E.E. au Conseil d'un règlement relatif à la libre circulation des travailleurs à l'intérieur de la Communauté. Doc. 128, October 10, 1967.

———. Report on preparations for the second session of the United Nations Conference on Trade and Development. Doc. 177, January 19, 1968.

———. Rapport sur les résultats de la deuxième session de la Conférence des Nations Unies sur le commerce et le développement. Doc. 86, July 1, 1968.

———. Proposition de résolution présentée par MM. Metzger, Vals, Wohlfart, Vredeling et Dehousse au nom du groupe socialiste sur la politique de la Communauté à l'égard du bassin méditerranéen. Doc. 202, January 23, 1969.

———. Rapport sur l'accord créant une association entre la C.E.E. et la République Tunisienne, l'accord créant une association entre la C.E.E. et le royaume du Maroc, les projets de règlements y relatifs. Doc. 48, May 28, 1969.

———. Rapport sur les propositions de la Commission des Communautés Européennes au Conseil (doc. 65/71) relatives à des règlements et des décisions concernant la mise en oeuvre des préférences généralisées en faveur des pays en voie de développement. Doc. 71/71, June 9, 1971.

Treaty Establishing the European Economic Community and Connected Documents. Luxembourg: Publishing Services of the European Communities, 1962.

Series Publications of European Community Institutions

Bulletin of the EEC Commission, monthly. Publishing Services of the European Communities.

Bulletin of the European Communities, monthly. Publishing Services of the European Communities.

European Community, monthly. European Communities Information Service, London.

European Community, monthly. European Communities Information Service, Washington.

European Documentation, A Survey, quarterly. European Parliament Secretariat, General Directorate of Parliamentary Information and Documentation.

Information Memos. Commission of the European Communities, Spokesman's Group.

Journal Officiel des Communautés Européennes. Publishing Services of the European Communities.

Press Releases. Commission of the European Communities, Spokesman's Group.

Speeches and Articles by Commission Officials

Raymond Barre. Address at the Fifth International Investment Symposium, Bellagio, June 2, 1970.

_____. "The Economic and Monetary Union: Its Objectives and its Problems." Statement to the European Parliament, Nov. 18, 1970. Bulletin of the European Communities, 1971, No. 1.

_____. "Building Economic and Monetary Union." Bulletin of the European Communities, 1971, No. 3.

Lionello Levi Sandri. "Free Movement of Workers in the European Community." Bulletin of the European Communities, 1961, No. 6.

_____. "The Role of Social Policy in European Integration." Address to the General Meeting of the Belgian Association for Social Progress, February 10, 1964.

_____. "Free Movement of Workers in the European Community." Bulletin of the European Communities, 1968, No. 11.

Sicco L. Mansholt. "Les agriculteurs à l'époque de la Mutation." Groningen, Feb. 16, 1968.

_____. Summary of the speech given on Dec. 10, 1968.

_____. "Towards New Guidelines for the Common Agricultural Policy."
Bulletin of the European Communities, 1971, No. 3.

Index

163

About the Author

Glenda Goldstone Rosenthal holds degrees from Oxford University, the College of Europe, and Columbia University. She received the Ph.D. in political science from Columbia in 1973 and has held teaching positions at Pace University, Vassar College, and Rutgers University. She is on the faculty of New York University and Baruch College of the City University of New York. Dr. Rosenthal is also a research associate of Columbia University's Institute on Western Europe and Yale University's Program on Problems of Advanced Industrial Societies. She has worked in various information capacities for Agence EUROPE in Luxembourg, the French Embassy Press and Information Service, and the European Community Information Service in New York.